Jean-Pierre Panouillé

CARCASSONNE

In the Days of the Siege

Translation by Janice Abbott
Drawings by Jean-Claude Golvin

caisse nationale
des monuments
historiques
et des sites

PRESSES DU CNRS

CARCASSONNE AT THE END OF THE MIDDLE AGES

This visualization is based on a drawing of 1462 (kept at the Bibliothèque Nationale, estampes VA 17), which has been interpreted and completed in the light of the latest historical and archeological research. The Cité is seen from the north-east. The Aude separates the fortress from the new bourg (founded under Saint Louis). The Cité was still one of the most important military fortresses of the kingdom. Drawing by Jean-Claude Golvin, 1992.

1 Porte Narbonnaise
2 Tour du Trésau
3 Tour du Moulin du connétable
4 Porte nord, or porte du bourg or de Rodez
5 Tour de la Porte rouge
6 Tour de la Poudre
7 « Donjons »
8 Tour Pinte
9 Porte est du château
10 Tour de la Justice
11 Porte d'Aude or de Toulouse
12 Avant-porte d'Aude
13 Tour de l'Inquisition
14 Tour carrée de l'Evêque
15 Tour du Grand Burlas
16 Tour Saint-Nazaire, porte sud, or porte du Razès
17 Eglise Saint-Nazaire
18 Tour de la Vade
19 Tour de la Peyre
20 Chemin couvert
21 Barbacane du château
22 Voie d'Aquitaine (voie romaine Narbonne-Toulouse)
23 L'Aude
24 Ville basse
25 Eglise Saint-Michel

Collection directed by
Jean-Claude Golvin

Already published:
From Lutetia to Paris

To be published:
Pont du Gard
Saint-Denis
The Castle of Angers
The Theatre of Bordeaux

© Presses du CNRS, Paris, 1992
ISBN : 2-87682-071-4
© Caisse Nationale des Monuments
Historiques et des Sites, Paris, 1992
ISBN : 2-85822-100-6

CONTENTS

OUR HERITAGE TODAY

The collection ''Patrimoine au présent'' (Our Heritage Today) is the result of the determination of the Caisse Nationale des Monuments Historiques et des Sites (The Office for Historical Monuments and Sites) and the Centre National de la Recherche Scientifique (National Centre of Scientific Research) to work together to offer the public a new vision of the country's historical buildings.

Each book is organised round a theme. In the case of Carcassonne, this theme is of course the defence of a town in the Middle Ages, the way in which attacks and sieges were met with, and how military architecture contributed to defence strategy. The book summarises the state of research on the subject, describes the important events in the history of the town, and analyses the different periods in the construction and development of the Cité, placing them in their geopolitical context. The descriptions of medieval attitudes and techniques, and the vivid accounts of men in action enrich our understanding of the Cité's past. Reference is continually made to the original sources, enabling the reader to go further in his search.

The drawings showing the monument at key periods in its development help our understanding of the architecture. The book is amply illustrated with documents, in some cases basic historical documents, in others, documents chosen to provoke the imagination. The photographs have all been selected both for their historical and aesthetic value.

The aim behind the collection ''Patrimoine au présent'' (Our Heritage Today) is to bring back the spirit of the places described, to breathe life into objects and stones, and to make the buildings live again, through the words of those who have studied them in depth.

Jean-Claude Golvin

The Cité seen from the south
*The two city walls surround
a town covering an area of approximately 25 acres.
In the west (on the left), the old Saint-Nazaire
cathedral and the castle. In the background,
the Black Mountains.*

THE REDISCOVERED FORTIFICATION

In November 1904, the Cité of Carcassonne was withdrawn from the list of protected military sites. The decision came as no surprise. It was no longer a fortress in the strict sense of the word and little military importance could be attached to the breached walls, to the roofless towers, to the lists cluttered with houses, sheds and vegetable gardens.

A ruin ready for demolition

Ville basse,
Plan 24

The Lower Town had started to pull down its ramparts; was the same true of the Cité? In fact, slowly and unobtrusively the dismantling had already begun. For years the crenellation stones had been there for the taking, and many had benefited from this excellent source of building materials for their new garden walls or houses. This slow erosion was in danger of turning into an earthquake. A number of important builders dreamt of emulating Palloy, the demolition contractor of the Bastille, and recuperating a vast stock of cut stone for their new building projects. They were quick to point out that the stones from the Cité could well be used to build a new hospital or to restore the island or Trivalle's spinning-mills, which had been partly destroyed by a flood of the River Aude. They emphasised the

danger presented by the shaky fortifications and pointed out that at any given moment part of the barricades might topple down on one of the houses and wipe out a, whole family. They criticised the lists as being insanitary. (The lists had become a throughfare with, of course, no form of drainage.) More than on hundred and twenty hovels, huddled against the precinct walls, accomodated the poorest of the town's weavers. They were tiny dwellings "dirty, dark and damp", as Docteur Villermé was to describe them a few years later in his inquest on the *Physical and moral state of workers* in France. The destruction of the fortifications would have the advantage of doing away with this belt of misery, which encircled a whole area itself hardly better off, and of decently rehousing the workers. The director of the domains listened favourably to these arguments and, for a give-away sum, he sold off parts of the city walls which, he claimed, were no more than ruins.

A monument worth saving

However not everybody agreed with this reasoning. The Préfet considered out that the damage was "more the result of criminals than the ravages of time". Questions

The West front, before and after restoration
The restoration mostly concerned repairs to the rooves and battlements.
A possible reconstruction : the little castle, which links the outside wall
with the castle buildings.

Bishop Radulphe's Tomb (upper section)
*The tomb, discovered by Cross-Mayrevieille
in 1839 in a chapel under the church
of Saint-Nazaire, was much admired
by Viollet-le-Duc.*

The Lists
*By 1891 the restorations were almost finished,
but the houses, which had been built against
be city walls during the period when
the fortifications were left derelict, had
not yet been demolished.*

were raised: "Shouldn't we be considering the walls as a historical monument worthy of conservation?" (Mazière, the town architect, November 1814). It was pointed out that the Cité had been an exceptional fortress. The double ramparts and the fifty "gothic" towers were still, luckily, practically intact, and symbolised an illustrious past. The fortifications, therefore, could be considered as a monument.

Ruins or monument? It should not be forgotten that the greater part of the edifice was still well and truly standing. On 1st August 1800, the army reclassified the Cité as a second-class fortress. This might almost be seen as an act of charity on its part, a way of saving respectable remains. The perimeter of the fortifications was inspected and repairs carried out.

In the period 1830-1850, various efforts were made, both at the local and the national levels, to save the "medieval city". In Paris, the Minister of the Interior appointed a General-Inspector of Historical Monuments, whose brief was to determine what needed to be done to ensure the protection of the country's historical monuments and to estimate the cost of such protection. Prosper Mérimée, who succeeded Ludovic Vivet in this post, travelled untiringly round France. He immediatley realised the importance of the Cité walls, which, he believed, constituted a fine example of late medieval Visigoth military architecture. He also drew attention to the originality of the Saint-Nazaire basilica, a half-Romanesque, half-Gothic building. The Commision of Arts and Sciences at Carcassonne, one of the first scientific societies founded in the provinces, and its young General Secretary Jean-Pierre Cross-Mayrevieille, fought for the listing of Saint-Nazaire and its fortifications. In 1839 Cross-Mayrevieille discovered the tomb of Bishop Radulphe buried beneath several cubic metres of earth in

Eglise
Saint-Nazaire,
Plan 17

Cité de CARCASSONNE
Lices au Sud Est
(Oct 91). J E D

a chapel. Viollet-le-Duc was later to write: "This tomb alone renders the pilgrimage to Carcassonne essential for archeologists."

Viollet-le-Duc at Carcassonne

In the following year Cross-Mayrevieille, now thirty years old, was appointed Inspector of Historical Monuments and representative of the Minister of the Interior for the Aude. The old cathedral was listed. It was in a pitiful state: during the Revolution the nave had been used as a barn for storing fodder and the north arm of the transept had housed the blacksmith's forge. The first works, carried out by the architect Champagne, were not particularly impressive. In 1844, Viollet-le-Duc was put in charge of the restoration. His preliminary report was enthusiastically acclaimed in the *Revue de l'Aude*, a periodical founded by Théophile Marcou and Jean-Pierre Cross-Mayrevieille, and which ardently defended "the arts".

From the year 1844, Viollet-le-Duc worked regularly on the Saint-Nazaire site. He wrote to his wife: "I am here the whole blessed day, surrounded by a lot of old women come to confess, who think nothing of passing their fleas on to me." Helped by a team of exceptional artists, including the sculptor Perrin, and a mainly local workforce, he set to work, first making a careful study of the Cité walls. He did not think very much of the operations carried out under the supervision of the army engineers. Cross-Mayrevieille and Mérimée agreed with him. On the surface it looked as though the fortifications were being saved, but in fact they were being disfigured.

In July 1859, the army once again took the fortifications off the list of protected monuments and put them over to the State. They had grown tired of maintaining the walls and towers to no purpose, and were aware that, in spite of the effort expended since 1820, one could not really talk in terms of real restoration. This was a godsend for the "demolition clan", who had never lost hope. At this point Cross-Mayrevieille launched a campaign to rally public opinion and obtained the support of the town council and most of the elected representatives of the department. His approach was suprisingly modern; he suggested that not only should the monument itself be saved, but the whole surrounding area. As early as August of the same year, the Minister of War, the Marquis d'Hautpoul, agreed to go back on his decision. Funds for the initial rescue operations and restoration had to be found, as well as the right people to implement them.

On 3rd October 1852, the Prince-Président, Louis-Napoléon, visited the Lower Town. In the evening, Jean-Pierre Crosse-Mayrevieille had the towers of the Cité illuminated with Bengal lights. The future Napoléon III was delighted with the spectacle, but refused to visit the fortifications the next day[1].

The following year, the first subsidies were granted by the central government. The decision as to who should be in charge of the works was the subject of long negotiations between the Ministry of War and the Ministry of the Interior. The competence and talent of Viollet-le-Duc eventually won the day. Initial work began in 1855. It was not long before the general public in Carcassonne began to appreciate the importance of the enterprise which had been undertaken. In November 1858, the town council awarded Viollet-le-Duc a gold medal for his "untiring zeal". These congratulations reveal that the former ruins had now become a prized heritage. In fact, through his scholarly writings, the architect had continuously emphasised and drawn the attention of Europe to the

Ville basse, Plan 24

profound significance of what might be a unique example of medieval military architecture.

The restoration works, conducted by Viollet-le-Duc until his death in 1879 and subsequently by his friend Boeswillwald and the architect Nodet, were almost completed by the beginning of the century. It had taken a particularly long time to clear the lists of all their parasite constructions. The expropriation procedures led to much petty bickering, even though most of the offers of compensation had been reasonable. In 1903, ninety-nine years after being abandoned in 1804, the fortifications were transferred from the Ministry of War to the Ministry of Fine Arts.

An authentic restoration?

Carcassonne is not a re-creation like Pierrefonds. The original parts make up about four-fifths of the monument as we know it today. The photographs taken be-

The Narbonne Gate in 1838
The main entrance to a town on the decline, or, in the words of Cross-Mayrevieille, to "a monument of military architecture unique in France". Engraving by Raynal.

The Church of Saint-Nazaire

In the foreground of this water-colour by Viollet-le-Duc, we see the West front of the Romanesque nave, which the architect decided to decorate with a crenellated terrace. The two arms of the transept can be seen in the background.

The Narbonne Gate

In general, Viollet-le-Duc distinguished restoration (the rooves) from reconstruction. For example, hoardings were only put up on parts of the castle wall.

fore the first restoration works confirm the accuracy of the detailed drawings made by Viollet-le-Duc. These show the fortifications from which only the upper parts are missing. Viollet-le-Duc considered, however, that "the building should be restored in its entirety". This point of view was opposed as early as the 19th century. "Unfortunately, wrote Taine, the surrounding walls have been repaired. The new clean constructions, so out of place today, look like an opera setting." The restorer turned his back on the romantic, rather silly passion for ruins; he was more intent on a didactic approach. He believed that a walk along the curtain walls with their restored battlements, or a view of the reconstructed hoardings on the east face of the castle, or a tour of the interior of a tower with its fireplace, its bread oven, ant its cistern, would bring the past to life better than any book. Moreover, it was absolutely essential to restore the roofing in order to protect the vaults from the rain, and in this case, a very strange ensemble would have resulted if the rest of the monument had been left as it was.

Viollet-le-Duc was well versed in the history of the Cité, and had an excellent command of the principles of siege warfare and medieval military architecture. With this background he took great pains to use the correct stonework for the successive construction periods. When restoring, he took his inspiration from other parts of the original building; when making additions he followed a certain logic, which, for example, led him to decide that a door should be protected by an overhanging brattice. His "rationalism" is undoubtedly rather remote from the medieval mind. His descriptions of the fortifications on the west of the castle and the barbican, or of the mechanisms of the Narbonne Gate, almost read like a series of equations, the result of which must be the inevitable defeat of the enemy. The

Barbacane du château, Plan 21

restoration works, however, do not entirely reflect the contents of the meticulously detailed "pedagogic" drawings and notes. There is a certain restraint, rather than the excess so often deplored.

Errors there are, however. It is unclear why the Romanesque nave of Saint-Nazaire should have been renovated in the form of a huge, monotonously shaped rectangle, when the original nave of the 12th century, still visible, was small and roughly square-shaped. The western crenellated bell-tower is, in the words of Marcel Durliat[2], "an abomination". There is no reason to suppose that the church was ever fortified. Lashed by the ever-present winds of Carcassonne, the sandstone chosen by Viollet-le-Duc has split more quickly than the original medieval stone. The exterior decoration of Saint-Nazaire, completely restored by Perrin, is already in a sorry state.

Eglise Saint-Nazaire, Plan 17

Viollet-le-Duc is not responsible for all the mistakes. For example, the fake drawbridge in front of the Narbonne Gate, of doubtful aesthetic and archeological value, is the work of Boeswillwald. The roofing has been the object of much controversy, many critics condemning the use of slate, considered a sacrilege in the *pays d'Oc*. It would seem that Viollet-le-Duc finally chose this building material for reasons of economy and because slate was easier to fix on the frame which had been designed a little on the steep side. As we shall see, the fortifications were largely the works of royal architects who had come from the north of the Loire, after the viscounty of Carcassonne was annexed to the Capetian domains. In general these northern architects used flat "*bourguignon*" tiles as a covering material. Viollet-le-Duc had been aware of this: in his first project he had planned to have Narbonne towers topped with glazed tiles.

Porte Narbonnaise, Plan 1

Should the restoration be restored? The question raised by the French section of

Icomos (International Council on Monuments and Sites) during a congress at Toulouse in April 1985 directly concerns Carcassonne. The architects in charge of historical monuments, who followed the masters of the 19th century, were above all pragmatic. On the north side, the towers of the outside ramparts had been given pepper-box rooves. The guard route which went round these rooves was open to the public at the beginning of this century. Many a visitor took away a slate tile as a souvenir, assuming that this would put them in possession of a relic from the far distant past. The slate rooves were replaced with cement slabs which protected the vaults and constituted no temptation to souvenir-hunters. The slate-topped Gallo-Roman towers, at least those on the north front, were recovered with a gently sloping, flute-tiled roofing, recalling the Gallo-Roman *tegulae* and *imbrices*. The great constructions of the 19th century such as the Trésau Tower and the Narbonne Gate were stripped of their slate and recovered with *bourguignon* tiles. Archeological research carried out in the same period confirmed that this correction was fully justified. The last restoration campaign concerned the Count's castle. In this case the restorers limited themselves to following the original as closely as possible. It is true that the dating of the castle fortifications, upon which any important alteration must depend, has still not been determined. Meanwhile, the work of Viollet-le-Duc has become part of the history of the Cité.

Tour du Trésau, Plan 2

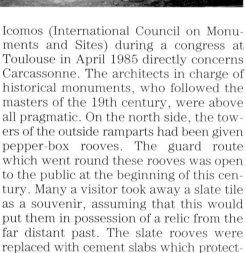

From 1908 onwards, the cinema...

As a change from painted backgrounds, Louis Feuillade came to the Cité to film le Serment des fiançailles *in a natural setting. The walls of the Cité were used by the film industry to represent the city walls of Orléans, as seen here in* la Merveilleuse Vie de Jeanne d'Arc, *those of Beauvais in* le Miracle des loups, *those of Budapest in* la Fiancée de Frankenstein, *and those of Nottingham in* Robin des Bois...

GEOGRAPHICAL AND HISTORICAL CONTEXT

"A major fortress and key to the Languedoc country." This was how King Charles VI described the Cité in 1408, thus eloquently summing up the mighty fortifications and the important strategic role of Carcassonne. The geographical position of the Cité might lead us to believe that its destiny was inevitable. But we should beware of such excessive determinism. History, as well as the hazards of geographical location explain a military vocation, which, far from being permanent, is dependent on events, on the balance of power between peoples, and on the will of sovereigns.

A strategic location

Carcassonne "locks up" two major routes. The first of these crosses what is sometimes know as the "Gallic Isthmus". Extending from Bordeaux to Narbonne, it is the shortest land connection linking the Atlantic with the Mediterranean. From Lower Languedoc in the East to the Aquitaine Basin in the West, it takes the narrow "Carcassonne corridor" bordered to the north by the edge of the Massif Central (the Black Moutains), and to the south by the foothills of the Pyrenees (the Corbières). The second route is the one linking the Iberian peninsula with the rest of Europe. It leads through the Aude valley towards the south, passing through Limoux, Quillan, Axat, to the mountain

L'Aude, Plan 23

paths and passes of the Pyrenees, and then on to Catalunia.

Carcassonne and its surrounding region acted as a buffer zone between the Atlantic region and the Mediterranean world, two geographical areas which, although differing profoundly and facing in different directions, had never quite turned their backs on each other.

This border role is reflected in the geography of the area. Just fifty kilometres west of Carcassonne, in the Naurouze moutain pass, one comes across a wateshed: on the one side, water flows down to the Atlantic Ocean, on the other, to the Mediterranean. And it is above Carcassonne that the continental and oceanic air masses converge with those from the Mediterranean, bringing fluctuating weather conditions to the region. Local expressions such as "le marin veut rentrer" (the *marin*, the moist wind from the south-east is going to blow), or "le cers va tenir" (the *cers*, the violent wind from the west, is here for a bit), bear witness to the eternal battle between the winds from the east and the west. And finally, it is in the region of Carcassonne that mixed farming and cereal growing give way to the vine and scrubland.

As we shall see, this natural border was a frontier between the royal kingdom of the Franks and the Visigoth kingdom of Spain. The other nearby frontier which comes readily to mind is that of the

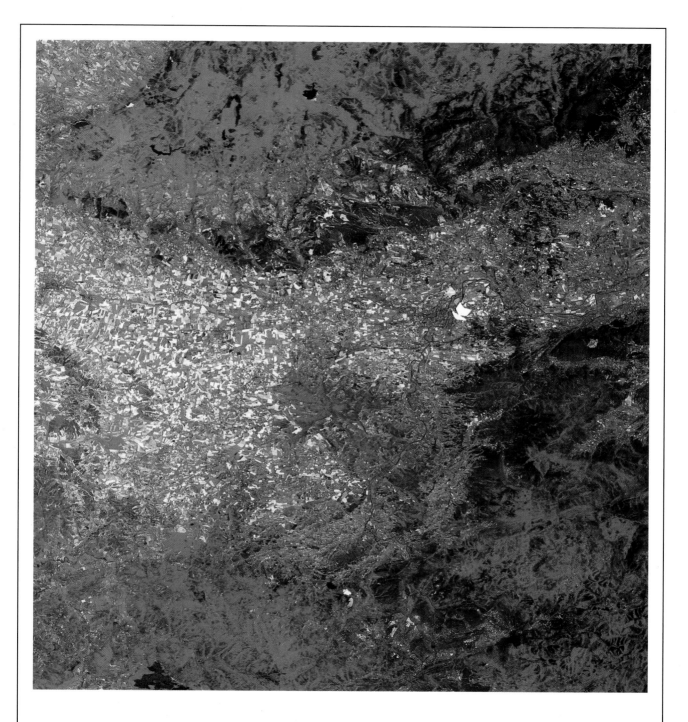

The Carcassonne Corridor, as seen by the SPOT 1 satellite

In the north, the forests (in red) and scrubland (darker) of the Black Mountains. In the south, the outlines of the Corbières. In the centre, the Carcassonne corridor, revealing the Aquitaine-type agriculture (small-holdings, mainly cereal-growing) ; in the south, the beginnings of the vine-growing area (darker).

Pyrenees, but for many years this natural frontier was nos a political one. Moreover, at the regional level, Carcassonne acted as a unifying force to the surrounding mosaic of widely differing landscapes: the Carcassonne plains, the limestone plateaux of the Minervois, the rocky, fissured Corbières, the gentle slopes of the Razès, the Maleperre hills, parts of the Lauragais plain, the Aude gorges, the heavy wooded relief of the Black Mountains.

A well-chosen site

Located on a rocky spur on the extreme edge of one of the last branches of the Corbières, the Cité is well adapted to the purposes of security and observation. The site, in spite of its low altitude (a little less than 460 feet high), offers a clear view of the Pyrenees, the Black Mountains and the plain which separates them. On the extreme west, the mound rises 150 feet above a meander of the Aude, before the latter turns direction to take the "Carcassonne corridor", through to the sea. On this side the relief is sheer. On the opposite side, the slope is not so steep, thus making access fairly easy. However, a trench solves this problem of defence.

L'Aude, Plan 23

The location seems ideal except perhaps for the size of the available area. It would, however, be wrong to assume that the site was used from ancient times. About five thousand years B.C., the peoples of this region began to settle down and turn to agriculture and animal rearing. Whereas we have evidence of neolithic villages very near the mound of the Cité around 3500 B.C. (Cavanac, Auriac, Berriac), the Cité itself appears to have been unoccupied. The first agglomeration, which might be termed Carcassonian, appeared round about the 8th century B.C. But it was on the site of Carsac, a little less than two kilometres from the Cité, that this settlement started and developed. Spread out on what was a huge area for prohistoric times, the village contained a mix of stock enclosures, wood and mud dwellings, small silos for family use, deep ditches (reserved for the community or for commercial use?), potters' kilns and smelters' furnaces, open spaces probably used for the exchange of local produce (ores, salvaged bronze objects for resmelting, cereals...) and importations from afar (wines from Greece and Etruria, Greek, Punic and Etruscan ceramics). The settlement was protected by V-shaped ditches, measuring twelve feet wide and six feet deep, and probably also, further back by banks made from excavated soil and by wooden stockades. For reasons unknown to us, the settlement of Carsac came to an end during the 6th century B.C. Yet it is from the middle of the same century that we have the first signs of occupation of the Cité mound.

It would seem reasonable to assume that there was a transfer of the settlement from the Carcas plateau up to the rocky spur of the Cité. The latter was a less spacious site (15 to 17 acres), but its geographical position made it good for defence, and it had an excellent view of the great Aquitaine route, rendering it ideal for observation purposes. This new settlement is typical of the perched villages, called *oppida*, a fairly widespread phenomenon in Languedoc at this period. The tendency might have been prompted by a need for greater security, or by a desire to observe more efficiently, and subsequently better exploit the increasing movements of exchange between the Mediterranean civilisations and those of the hinterland.

Voie d'Aquitaine, Plan 22

A Roman town on the Aquitaine route

The four centuries separating the beginning of the *oppidum*, forerunner of the

Cité, from the Roman Conquest, reflect how Carcassonne's position exposed it to different influences: from across the Pyrenees with the long Iberian ascendancy, from the Celts with the apparently uneventful invasion of the Volques Tectosages, and finally from the Italians due to a very active trade preceeding the arrival of the armies of Dometius Aenobarbus. The annexation of the Mediterranean region of Gaul by the Romans, and the foundation in 118 B.C. of the colony of Narbonne extending as far as Toulouse, do not seem to have provoked much

The west side

It was possible to do without a ditch on the side of the hill near the river, since the slope was particularly steep here. In the bottom right we see the Aude rising.

The Roman town

*The threshold and some mosaic
remains from the 1st century, discovered
under the courtyard and buildings in
the north-west part of the castle.
In the background, the foundations
of the apse of the seigneur's chapel.*

resistance. Was the *oppidum*, set on the Cité mound, protected as it had originally been, by a system of ditches and banks? Had it been surrounded by a wall of great stone blocks as at Pech Mao near Sigean or at Enserune? Were these defences put to use, or, as is more likely, was the Roman presence easily accepted? It is difficult to give a definitive reply. At all events the "Romanisation" took place gradually: an administrative framework was established, thus giving support to Italian traders, but without brutally destroying the bases of the old Iberian and Celtic cultures.

The oldest mention of the name Carcassonne, or more precisely of the latin *Carcasone (Carcaso, Carcasonis)*, appears in the *Pro Fonteio* of Cicero. In about the year 70 B.C. the famous Roman lawyer defended the *praetor* Fonteius, who had been accused by the taxpayers of Narbonne of levying excessive taxes, especially on the jars of Campanian wine sent to Gaul. A duty was levied at several points, one of which was *Vulchalone*. According to Monseigneur Elie Griffe[3] works, *Vulchalone* is probably the alteration in a later manuscript of the word *Carchasone*.

Archeological excavations have revealed the existence of a small prosperous town extending on the north side to the foot of the *oppidum*. As a result of the security provided by Roman discipline and of the demands of commerce (sufficient area, ease of access), a second settlement grew up at the top of the hill. The colonia *Julia Carcaso* was founded a quarter of a century before our era, freeing the region from the administrative tutelage of Narbonne. But under the Middle Empire Carcassonne did not expand in the same way as Narbonne or Toulouse. A few remains of walls covered with a painted coating and some fragments of mosaics bear witness to the existence of fairly handsome buildings in various parts of the Cité (the Count's Castle, the south wing, in the area around the Narbonne Gate), but so far, no trace of a great public monument has been found.

We know practically nothing about Carcaso during the long *Pax Romana*. Some historians claim that it was a small regional capital (Jean-Pierre Cross-Mayrevieille). Others are convinced of the "mediocre status of Carcassonne at the height of the Roman occupation", a "fortress (the former *oppidum* turned military post) flanked by its little bourg" (Joseph Poux). But Guy Rancoule, in the chapter written by him of l'*Histoire de Carcassonne* published under the direction of Jean Guilaine and Daniel Fabre, is certainly right in suggesting something mid-way between the extremes, that of "a small, very busy town", greatly benefiting from the Narbonne-Toulouse Roman road, which passed immediately below the

**Porte
Narbonnaise,
Plan 1**

**Voie
d'Aquitaine,
Plan 22**

The setting
*The last bulge of the Corbières, before the narrow plain, which separates
them from the Black Mountains, visible in the background. The Cité towers
150 feet above the Aude. It is here that the river turns east from the
north-south course it has followed from its source in the Pyrenees, and flows
on to the Mediterranean.*

oppidum and crossed the settlement flanking the hill to the north[4].

The Later Empire: a period of insecurity

The 3th century brought with it power struggles, the beginning of the *bagaudes* (bands of insurgent peasants and deserting soldiers attacking the "richs"), and the first two waves of invasions, one in 257, bringing the Franks to the south-west and then to Spain, the other in 275 during which, according to the chroniclers, the Germans occupied about sixty cities. All these factors led to an increasing fear of attack and a desire for security. In the last quarter of the century, many towns built defence walls.

This obsession with security continued

Love crowned with vine branches

This piece of sculpture, which was found near Carcassonne, bears witness to the quality of local art during the Pax Romana.

into the beginning of the 4th century, when Constantine ordered the organisation of a "thorough" defence system throughout the Empire. In general, there was a distinct reduction in the living space occupied, in order to reduce the area that had to be defended.

And what about Carcassonne in all this? Most of the walls and towers of today's inner ramparts, particularly those on the north front, look like Gallo-Roman constructions of the Later Empire, with their characteristic small stonework alternating with chains of brick and their semi-circular turrets pierced with windows. The comparison has often been made with the walls of Senlis or Le Mans, still visible today. In the absence of written sources or archeological discoveries to provide us with precise dating, it seems logical to assume that the population of Carcassonne, the majority of whom undoubtedly lived just below the mound and along the Aquitaine route, took refuge in the rocky spur of the Cité and participated in the general urban fortification movement taking place in Gaul.

In 333, Carcassonne is referred to as a *castellum* in the account of a journey of a pilgrim travelling from Bordeaux to Jerusalem. The idea of fortification is clear; the same term is used for Le Mans where the surrounding walls, similar to those of the Cité, encircled a slightly larger town (1,500 yards in perimeter compared with 1,000 at Carcassonne). Le Mans was also situated on a hill overlooking a river (the Sarthe). At the beginning of the 4th century, or more probably in the second half of the 3th century, according to William Rancoule, the town was contained within the same area that it occupies today (scarcely more than 17 acres), surrounded by a wall flanked with towers.

The second city wall, the outside one, was not built until the 13th century. At this time, the inner wall was also partly

Voie d'Aquitaine, Plan 22

rebuilt-in general following the original groundplan, and partly patched up.

On the borders of the Visigoth kingdom of Spain

The first historians of the Cité, Jean-Pierre Cross-Mayrevieille, Viollet-le-Duc and Joseph Poux, considered that the original fortress was the work of the Visigoths. This thesis can scarcely be defended on archaelogical grounds, except for the argument put forward by Yves Bruand[5]. He points to the irregular arrangement of the chains of brickwork, which contrast sharply with the strict order found on most of the Later Empire walls, and which might be seen as "a later re-use of debased Roman techniques". The oval shape of the walls, which follows the profile of the spur they encircle, seems unusual; in general, Gallo-Roman builders preferred a square or rectangular layout. But it is the strategic importance of Carcassonne in the 6th century which provides the best argument for the theory that the Cité fortifications are of Visigoth origin — if not actually built by the Visigoths themselves, at the very least constructed under their orders by the local population who still more or less remembered the building techniques used during the Later Roman Empire.

At the beginning of the 5th century, Gaul was invaded by the Visigoths, the Franks and the Burgundians. The Visigoths occupied the West and the South from the Loire to Provence; fifty years later they were to invade and extend their rule over Spain. The Visigoth domination was soon upset by the expansion of the Franks. In 507 Alaric II was defeated at Vouillé (near Poitiers) by Clovis and killed in combat. Toulouse, the capital of the Visigoth kingdom, was taken by the Franks. The following year Clovis laid siege to Carcassonne. The episode is men-

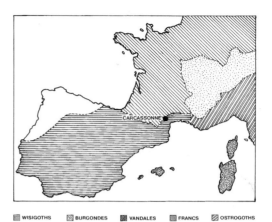

WISIGOTHS   BURGONDES   VANDALES   FRANCS   OSTROGOTHS

tioned by Procope de Cesaree, a Byzantine author living in the middle of the 6th century. "They laid siege to Carcassonne with great zeal, since they had been told that it contained the royal treasure which Alric the Elder had looted when he seized Rome. Part of this booty was the treasure store of Solomon, the King of the Hebrews, a collection of exceptional beauty."

According to Procope, the arrival of Theodoric, the King of the Goths of Italy, with his powerful army, terrified the Franks, who raised the siege. This passage, taken from a somewhat unreliable author, was not lost on the 19th century intellectual elite of Carcassonne. They founded an association with the declared aim of drying out the big well of the Cité and recovering the invaluable treasure.

At the beginning of the 6th century and for more than two hundred years to come, Carcassonne became a frontier town on the northern limits of a Visigoth empire. This empire originated in Spain and spread across the Pyrenees, and through the whole of Bas-Languedoc, which at that

Franks and Visigoths
Septimanie (Languedoc), the last territorial possession of the Visigoths in Gaul, was defended by Carcassonne.

time was called Septimanie. In 585, the grandson of Clovis, Gontran, King of Burgundy, launched an offensive in the direction of the Mediterranean. One of his armies appeared before Carcassonne. According to Gregory of Tours, the population opened the gates without resisting, but "There was some conflict or the other with the people of Carcassonne, and they (Gontran's men) left the town. Then Terentiolius, former count of the town of Limoges, fell, struck by a stone thrown down from the wall. In 587 the Cité was again unsuccessfully besieged by the Frankish Duke Didier. The following year, an army sent by Gontran was ambushed "near a small river in the vicinity of the town" (the Aude or its tributary, the Fresquel).

L'Aude, Plan 23

The attitudes adopted by the chroniclers are as revealing as the battles they describe. Gregory of Tours has Gontran say: "First of all, give us the control of the province of Septimanie near the Gauls, since it is an indignity that the frontiers of these horrible Goths should extend into the territory of the Gauls." Isidore of Seville, in the opposite camp, describes the victory won over Boson as "the greatest that the Visigoths had ever won in the Spains". The plural form is used to include the regions on both sides of the Pyrenees. So we see that the Franks did not consider the "Carcassonne corridor" as a frontier, and the Visigoths did not want the Pyrenees to be one. The Gallo-Roman basis of the Cité population seem to have been indifferent to these quarrels and quite happy to be dominated by either side, preferring perhaps the Catholic Franks to the Arian Visigots, until the Visigoth king was converted to catholicism in 987 and established Carcassonne as a bishopric.

Yves Bruand considers that the building of the inner walls of the Cité can probably be dated to the end of the 6th century. The walls would have been put up to resist the Frankish agressors. However, there is no conclusive archeologica evidence to support this thesis. In the absence of irrefutable evidence, it is probably wiser to continue to see the walls as a monument of the 3th century. But the debate goes on and there is no doubt that the key position occupied by Carcassonne in the 6th century would have justified important fortification works. For more than a century to come, the town would belong to an empire from across the Pyrenees, and would act as a defence line to that empire.

Between Toulouse and Barcelone

At the beginning of the 8th century, the Arab invasion brought to an end the Visigoth kingdom of Spain. First, probably in 713, Carcassonne fell to the Saracens, following a raid rather than a full scale conquest. The Arab chronicler who mentions this episode waxes lyrical over the seven columns of silver decorating the church of Our Lady of "Carchachouna". This wealth, even if somewhat exagerated, is indicative of the vitality of the settlement spread out over the north side of the hill. Excluding times of extreme insecurity, the town had always harboured a large population. In 725 the town was again besieged and taken; this time, it remained occupied for the next thirty years. In the middle of the 8th century, the Franks led by Pépin the Short, expelled the Arabs from Septimanie.

Little is known about the Cité during the Carolingian period. With the creation across the Pyrenees of a "Spanish March" including Catalunia and Navarre, Carcassonne was now a long way from the frontiers of the empire. Among the very few clues we have for this period, we find a few texts written a little before 900, which use the expression "civitate Carcas-

The Avar Postern
This is the only Later Empire wall gate still in use today.
Two ''Cyclopean'' blocks frame the passage-way. A discharging arch in brick
and sandstone voussoir relieves the lintel.

sonne'', citadel (cité) of Carcassonne. This title was to be used more and more, and gradually replaced the word town or any other way of referring to the citadel. From about 1000 A.C., we also have the first references to the church of Saint-Michel, and to a village of the same name termed *"castellare"*, located on the south side of the hill. History is no more eloquent on the subject of the first counts — Arfred, Oliba I, Oliba II (probably from Toulouse), Arnaud, or Roger of Couserans-Comminges... The marriage of Ermengarde of Couserans-Comminges with Raymond-Bernard Trencavel brought together an important territorial principality covering Carcassonne and the Razès (the region of Rennes-le-Château and Limoux), Albi and Nîmes, as well as the viscounty of Béziers and the seigneury of Agde. But it would seem that the couple preferred a more tangible, solid form of riches; in 1067 they relinquished their rights over Carcassonne and Razès and in return for 5,000 ounces of gold made Raymond Béranger I, Count of Barcelona, the seigneur of Carcassonne and its bourgs. Once again, the destiny of the Cité seemed linked with that of Spain. The transaction reveals the interest felt by the Catalan princes for Carcassonne, but it was not to last a long time. Ermengarde and her son, Bernard Aton, were not particularly chivalrous. When disorders broke out fol-

The seigneur's residence

This was the main room of the "big dungeon". The objects on display bring to mind the Carolingian and Roman periods. There is a particularly beautiful fountain, dating from the second half of the 12th century (from Lagrasse or Fontfroide).

lowing the assassination of Raymond Béranger II at Carcassonne in mysterious circumstances, Bernard Aton was quick to offer his services to guarantee the peace. He set himself up in the Cité and promised to restore the young heir of Raymond Béranger II when he came of age. This of course he later refused to do.

On three occasions the Counts of Barcelona attempted to recover their possession. These attempts provoked the Cité inhabitants to rebel and for several years they refused Raymond Aton entrance to their town. With the support of the Count of Toulouse, Raymond Aton finally triumphed and harshly punished the ''traitors''. In 1137 as a result of a marriage alliance bringing together the county of Barcelona and the kingdom of Aragon, Catalunia, counting in addition its territories in Provence, became one of the great powers in the South. This, in spite of its repeated failures over the Carcassès. The other great power was the county of Toulouse. The two houses were rivals in their ambitions for territorial expansion. The Trencavel cleverly exploited this rivalry to prevent either side from extending its domination over the entire South. Situated in the middle of an area of resistance, Carcassonne was ruled by a family who knew exactly how to profit from the ties of lordship when it suited them, and just as well how to empty those ties of any meaning when they sensed that their independence was threatened. This feudal imbroglio linking the houses of Toulouse and Barcelone resulted in an almost continuous state of warfare, with skirmishes, rapid *chevauchées* and taking of pledges. This state of affairs was all the more disastrous since each side employed bands of roving mercenaries who were responsible to no-one in particular, and who, when not needed by either of the two antagonists, pillaged on their own account. By the end of the 12th century, the

situation had apparently calmed down. The houses of Toulouse and Barcelona stopped squabbling and drew together; as for the Trencavel, it would seem that they had finally been adopted by their subjects. Revolts and plots became things of the past, and when the young Viscount Raymond-Roger opposed the Crusaders, he was able to count on the fidelity, the esteem and even the affection of his vassals and of the people of Carcassonne.

The Albigensian Crusade

The Council of Tours of 1163 and the Lateran Council of 1179 firmly condemned Catharism, and ordered that severe measures be taken to halt the spread of the heresy. The ''damnation'', as the heresy was called at the time, had a stronger hold in Languedoc than in any other region. The task of pursuing and arresting the heretics and avoiding further proselytism fell to the lay world, that is to say, to the seigneurs in possession of political power and an armed force. But in the South, many feudal lords were themselves Cathars. Peyre de Brens, Seneschal of the Trencavel for the region of Albi, Étienne de Servian in the Biterrois, Bertrand de Saissac, one of Roger II's companions, are all examples. Others, out of indifference or calculation, defied the authority of the Church, which had been given a new lease of life by the Gregorian reforms, and let ''good men'' go free. According to Peter of Vaux-de-Cernay, ''almost all the barons had become the defenders of heretics, they welcomed them into their home, they loved them fervently, they defended them against God and Church.'' The Cathars were able to keep to their ''school of heresy'', to preach, to take part in ''public debates'' where they sometimes had the better of their catholic opponents. In 1207 the legate Peter of Castelnau excommunicated the Count of Toulouse, a "protector" of heretics. On 14th January 1208, the legate was assassinated; Innocent III called for a Crusade. Raymond VI who was the most threatened by the Pope's declaration, first tried to form an alliance with Trencavel, then made due amends. The excommunication was lifted, and for good measure the Count of Toulouse took the Cross, thus turning the Crusaders against the Trencavel: "They counted on taking Toulouse, but the town made its peace. They say they will now take Carcassonne and Albi" (Crusade song). Carcassonne was the centre of Cathar proselytism; was it not even whispered that the town had had a Cathar bishop as well as a Catholic bishop for the last few years? The town therefore became the main target of the Crusaders.

THE CATHARS

The origins of the Cathar heresy most probably date back to the very ancient oriental doctrines developed in Persia by Zarathoustra in about the 7th century B.C., and by Manes or Mani in the 3rd century A.D. In the Middle Ages, Manicheisme, or the teachings of Manes, which described the world as the permanent confrontation between Good (God) and Bad (the devil), had a large following in the Balkans. Merchants, pilgrims, and Crusaders, who increasingly crossed these regions, discovered the religious dualism of those known as Bogomiles or Bougres (Bulgars). The wave sweeping through Western Europe, Northern Italy, the Rhineland, Flanders, Champagne as well as through the whole of Languedoc, was not just a heresy, it was more like a new religion. Although the followers of this religion were no more numerous in Albi than in other towns of the South-West, it was the name "Albigensian" that was applied to the followers of this new doctrine. The Cathars believed that there are two worlds, one, the work of God, consisting of invisible and immaterial beings, the other, the work of the devil, consisting of visible and material beings. Man is the fruit of this double genesis, his soul aspires to reach the heavenly universe, his body, a carnal straightjacket, keeps him prisoner. A "sacrament", the *consola-* *tum,* consisting of a simple laying on of hands, enables the soul to escape from the successive reincarnations in which evil keeps it. The *consolamentum* bestows purity (from the Greek word *catharos*), which alone opens the doors of the kingdom of God. Those who have received the sacrament must renounce all form of temporal satisfaction, while waiting for the supreme deliverance. They must possess nothing, must observe chastity and be strict vegetarians. Those who do not feel they have the force of character to lead such an ascetic existence may receive the *consolamentum in extremis*, at the end of their life. Jean-Louis Biget has demonstrated that only part of the population of Languedoc had been won over to Catharism in the 12th and 13th centuries.

The danger to the Catholic Church lay more in the quality of these "heretics" than in their number. In the towns the Cathars often belonged to the local elite: notaries, merchants, lawyers, knights. In the countryside the simple life-style, the honesty and courage of those known as the "good men" made them so popular, that the majority of the population who were Christian were not hostile to them. Many lords were openly in favour of them, either out of anti-clericalism or out of conviction.

The Cabaret castles (Lastours)
Peter Roger de Cabaret, Trencavel's advisor during the 1209 siege, opened his lands as a place of refuge to the heretics and the «good men».

FIGHTING MEN, ARMS AND WAR ENGINES

"Upon my word, it was a marvellous great army, twenty thousand knights, armed from head to foot..." The author of the Song of the Albigensian Crusade liked to talk in figures and he loved to multiply them. When the Crusading army was besieging Carcassonne, the Viscount Trencavel suggested to his barons that he make a sortie "with 400 of them". Later he went to parley "with an escort of 100 knights". The aim was to impress the audience, not to give a realistic account. The feudal public was, in any case, little concerned about exact figures. Numbers were part of the decor, and they had to be as impressive as possible, with a few great lords standing out: the Duke of Burgundy, the Count of Nevers, the Count of Saint Pol, the King of Aragon, Trencavel, Simon de Montfort, not forgetting a few high ranking ecclesiastics: the Archbishop of Sens, the Bishops of Autun and of Clermont, the Abbot of Cîteaux...

Beside the knights, or rather overshadowed by them, stood the villeins, more than 200,000, according to William of Tudèle, who was never niggardly in his estimates of the crowd. The infantry was made up of squires and sergeants-at-arms, but also civilians — peasants and burgesses who had taken the cross. We know nothing about what happened to them during the expedition. We have very few documents which might give us a more precise idea of the size of medieval armies. We are mostly left to make subtle deductions, risky calculations and extrapolations, only to end up making hypotheses. According to a charter of 1191, the Trencavel were the lords of a good sixty vassals in the viscouties of Béziers and Carcassonne alone. The seigneuries of Albi and Razès (the region of Limoux, Quillon, Montréal), which were also under the lordship of the Trencavel, would have owed much the same number of vassals. If we include the Lauragais, the Cabardès, the Minervois and the Terménès, we can reasonably total up some 200 knights, half of which might have participated in the defence of the Cité during the siege of 1208.

Fighting men

There were undoubtedly more lords among the Crusaders. We might make a comparison with the battle of Bouvines some five years later. On this occasion, the army assembled by Philippe Augustus was an unusually large one, numbering about 1,300 knights. It is unlikely that the noble contingent of the Crusaders' army was a big as this. From a numerical point of view, the body of mounted knights constituted but a small part of the army. The custom was that each lord be accompanied by a squire serving his apprenticeship before being dubbed a knight, and by one or two "boys" or "valets" who served their master, looked after his supplies, saw to the horses, set up camp and in

The towers of the Count's Castle
*Under the rule of the royal seneschals, the Treencavel's residence became
the centre piece of an extremely important fortress.*

their own way took part in the combat by guarding the prisoners, recuperating the equipment of unseated cavalry and collecting arms which had fallen on the battleground. Then there were the numerous sergeants, who were sometimes mounted, but more often on foot, crossbowmen, archers, pike-bearers and sometimes a few artisans (blacksmiths, carpenters, saddlers...). Finally, the use of roving mercenaries, prepared to offer their services to whoever paid them the most, became common. When calculating the size of an army we should probably multiply the number of knights by four or six, and in this way we arrive at a force of several thousand men. However, when estimating the forces taking part in a siege, we should not limit ourselves to counting the armed men, at least not when calculating those on the defence. The Cité and its bourgs sheltered three to four thousand people, added to which there were the refugees from the surrounding countryside. Civilians certainly took part in the defence, but their excessive numbers often constituted a hindrance rather than a help. It is difficult to know what to conclude from all this, except perhaps, that the Crusaders were three to four times more numerous than their opponents. In the words of the papal legates accompanying the Crusaders, their army was so huge "that it would seem that here has never been its equal in the Christian world". Time was also an important factor. The armies of the Middle Ages were transitory, and the control of timing, so essential in all strategy, was often lacking. The three months feudal service owed by vassals in Charlemagne's time had been reduced to 40 days. Once this obligatory

Recumbent statue of a knight
*The hauberk, or coat of mail, protected the head, neck and most of the body.
It was covered with a linen tunic bearing the knight's "coat of arms", too disfigured
in this case to enable us to identify the owner. 13th century, Lagrasse.*

period of duty had passed, the knights had to be paid. In addition, the sergeants-in-arms, the foot-soldiers, the archers and the crossbowmen were also paid, even if very poorly. They received between a tenth and a twelfth of the sum given to the knights, or to make another comparison, the same amount as the unskilled workers. Then there were the mercenaries, the Brabançons, Aragoneese, Navarrais, Catalans, Basques, Germans — so many names, almost always designating foreigners who came cheap. But these rootless bands, who feared neither God nor man, were never so happy as when looting and gloating over the fires they had caused.

The Crusade was to extend beyond the year 1209 partly because of the unfixed nature of the armies which assembled in the spring or the beginning of summer and broke up in the autumn, leaving a handful of helpless men to exploit the victory until there was total peace. This is exemplified by the difficulties of Simon de Montfort outside Toulouse from October 1217 to July 1218. His determination was to coast him his life. A big stone projected from one of those siege engines which we shall describe further on, struck him on the head and crushed his face. Although protected by a steel helmet "his eyes, his brain, his front teeth, his forehead and his jaw were smashed to pieces" (William of Tudèle). The blow was fortuitous but of such violence that none of the devices used by the knights to protect themselves from injury or death could have deflected it.

The knight equipment

Great progress had been made in the techniques of protecting knights from mortal blows, so that by the beginning of the 13th century, the knight who had sufficient means was an iron-clad man. The head

was protected by a helmet, the latest version of which was elongated and closed in, much like a cylindrical box, padded inside and perced with slits for the eyes and tiny holes for breathing. The helmet was abominably hot to wear and weighed down on the cervical vertebra since the helmet had not yet become long enough to rest on the shoulders. For this reason, when they were not on the battlefield, the knights wore a simple "iron hood". The hauberk covered most of the body. Known today as the "coat of mail", it was more frequently called a "coat of iron" in medieval times. This coat, made of interlaced iron rings, about one centimetre in diameter, reached down to the knees. From the hips downwards there was a slit in front and behind to enable the knight to mount his horse. The sleeves sometimes ended in a kind of mitten. Accord-

Knights (end of the 12th and beginning of the 13th century)

Reconstructed from seals. The knight's equipment consisted of a hauberk, a helmet covering the whole face, a shield bearing the arms, a sword and an axe.

ing to Viollet-le-Duc, this coat weighed about ten kilos (22 pounds). It was worn over a *gambison* or *gamboison,* a padded shirt, and under a *cotte d'armes,* a cloth tunic. From the first quarter of the 13th century the knights began to have their coats-of-arms represented on the tunic... The legs were covered in mail hose, the feet protected by iron shoes.

With this equipment, the risk of injury was reduced and feats of valour not quite so dangerous. In fact, it may partly explain the emergence of courage and daring as important knightly virtues. The less wealthy lords made do with a simpler version of the helmet which sometimes had a long piece coming down to protect the nose or the neck, and a shorter, more rigid hauberk, made of flat, filled-in rings of metal stuck on to a garment of leather or

The Castle Round Room

The room may have got its name from its semi-circular vaulting, or because meetings were held there in a circle.

thick cloth. Medieval armies often had a motley appearance, reflecting the differing abilities of each and everyone to equip themselves in the latest fashion. Now that the body was well protected, the shield became smaller. It was triangular in shape and the point turned towards the bottom was rounded in almond fashion. Fighting armour consisted first of a lance, to which the more powerful barons attached their banners, hence the name ''knight-banneret'' (vassals were only allowed a smal flag, the pennon), and one or two swords of different weight and length for cutting and thrusting, the longer sword being attached to the saddle. As the etymology of the word *chevalier* indicates, the knight only knew how to fight when mounted. For this reason, siege warfare with its protected terrace works, its long-distant exchanges of arrows, quarrels and stones, its assaults ressembling escalades and obstacle races more than anything else, did not much appeal to him. Moreover, he was deprived of the advantage of being mounted and the pleasure of caracoling. He had to have three mounts: a war horse or *destrier,* a palfry for travelling and a *roncin* or packhorse for transporting his goods. The horse was a precious possession and one taken from a lord, who fell during a tournament, or one snatched from the battlefield, was greatly prized. The Crusaders were overjoyed at the number of horses that the defeated were forced to abandon after the taking of Carcassonne. In some cases, the reimbursement of horses lost or crippled during the battle was planned.

The arbalet

Although they knew how to use the bow and the crossbow, the knights were not particularly partial to these weapons, which avoided physical combat and killed in an underhand manner. Their use

against Christians had been condemned at the end of the 11th century by Urban II and by the Lateran Council of 1139. The crossbow in particular was much feared. Although known in ancient times, it had largely been forgotten in the Early Middle Ages. It reappeared towards the end of the 11th century, but was little used in France for the next hundred years. Then in about 1200 it suddenly came to the fore. Indeed it was improved in a number of ways. The crossbowman could now slip his foot into a stirrup attached to the end of his crossbow before bending the bow. Some crossbowmen had a hook attached to their belt, which they used to pull the cord as they stood up. Later on, an even better form of the arm was constructed, this time with mechanisms which considerably increased the tension, such as the *pied-de-biche*, based on a lever principle, the lathe based on the winch principe, the jack or *cranequin* combining gears and toothed racks. But there were also disadvantages to this arm: it was heavy — an ordinary crossbow weighing 7 to 8 kilos (14 to 17 pounds), slow to load, and it made those who used it on the battlefield an easy target for the archers who could engage in action more rapidly. On the other hand, the crossbow was excellent for defence purpose. Safely positioned behind the walls pierced with arrow-slits and the crenellation merlans, the soldier could take his time, and correctly adjust his aim. In these circumstances, the power and range of the crossbow accomplished miracles.

Many other arms were used in the 13th century. There was an increase in the

Knightly combat

Detail of a mural painting which decorated the vaults of the Round Room.
The date of the painting is uncertain: middle of the 12th or beginning
of the 13th century.

different kinds of bows employed. The *turquoi* bow, probably imported from the Holy Land, was, with its accolade curvature, particularly effective. The knights wielded the axe and club, whereas the infantrymen used all kinds of hooked instruments to catch hold of and bring the cavalry down to the ground. Finally, there were slings and staff-slings known in ancient times as ''fustibals''. Modestus decribed them in the following way: ''A staff, a foot long, with a leather sling attached, which could project big stones, when propelled with both hands.''

War machines known in Antiquity

Described by Vitruvius and later by Vegetius or Ammien Marcellin, they facilitated four kinds of operations: that of ''bombarding'' the enemy by means of ballistas, catapults, scorpions or onagers, that of taking from the adversary the advantage of command, or rather of a dominating position, by using mobile wooden towers, that of approaching the wall while protected by wooden panels on rollers (the *plutei*, matlets) or galleries (vines), and that of demolishing the wall with battering-rams or by mining. ''An underground gallery is dug up to the town walls... When the sappers get to the foundations of the wall, they dig beneath it along a certain length, shoring it up with dry wood props which they surround with vine shoots and different combustible materials. The troops are then put in position for the assault, and the props are lit. The result is that the wall suddenly collapses creating a large breach'' (Vegetius). The Latin term used to designate these galleries, *cuniculi*, brings to mind the image of a rabbit digging into its burrow. The use of these war engines and devices had not been totally lost as a result of the barbarian invasions, but had become rare.

They were given a new lease of life in the 12th century. There are numerous reasons for this revival: the contact via the Crusades with civilisations where the construction techniques of such machines had continued and probably improved, the increasing importance of towns from a strategic point of view, larger, better-structured armies with more means at their disposal. It can also be explained by the fact that fortifications were now more solid and more elaborate. Finally, with the reduction in the length of feudal service, it was necessary to get things done quickly. It was one aspect of an intellectual renaissance, which, as Jean Gimpel[6] has shown, was both philosophic and scientific. The texts of Euclid, Archimedes, Heron of Alexandria and Ptolemy were translated, either directly form the Greek original or from their Arab translation. The Roman author Vegetius (rather than Vitruvius, who was very ''technical'' and difficult to understand), was very popular for his texts on the military arts. He was plagiarized and annotated and there was a proliferation of manuscripts. Philippe Contamine[7] cites the case of the Bishop of Auxerre, Hugues of Noyers (1183-1206): ''He loved to assemble a crowd of knights and to discuss military questions with them. He frequently reread Vegetius, who wrote about such matters, and he explained to the knights many precepts taken from this writer.'' The fashion continued into the 13th century. Feudal lords could usually read and write, but knew no Latin. Nevertheless they wanted to have access to the text.

Jean de Meung, translator of Vegetius

Among the works of Jean de Meung, the continuator of the *Roman de la Rose*, we find: *Le livre de Végèce, de l'art de la chevalerie, [...], en l'an Mil deux cent quatre vingt et quatre*. Jean de Meung gets lost in the Roman bestiary; the mining galeries are called *conninières*, rabbit warrens (*conin* = rabbit in medieval French), the ram becomes a sheep and the tortoise *bélière* (ram-tortoise, i.e. a ram protected by a double-sided roof) becomes a snail which "looks like a real snail, and, like the snail alternately draws in its feelers and sticks them out again". The small devices used to protect those whose job it was to bring earth and faggots to fill in the ditches, were no longer mice or little fish (*musculi* in Latin), but muscles. The translation sometimes has frankly no relationship at all with the real sense of the text. Tormenta, for example, which are spring-based missiles (made of bundles of tightly twisted ropes) become "*tourmens pour pugnier les malfaiteurs*" (torments to punish evil-doers), and bitumen (inflammable naphta) is changed into cement. The poet seems no more gifted in mathematics. The principle of the rule of three is not understood in this tip given by Vegetius of how to measure the height of a wall or tower: "When the sun makes the shadow of the towers and the walls fall obliquely on the ground, the shadow can be measured without the besieged noticing anything. A ten-foot rod can then be planted in the ground and its shadow measured. It is easy to calculate from the relation of one shadow to the other the height of the walls, once one knows how much shadow is thrown by a certain height." Jean de Meung is right to suggest the measuring of the shadows of the walls and the towers, but he forgets to talk of the staff, which serves as a standard, and one has the impression that he considers the length of the shadow equal to the height of the walls. On the other hand he loves to pepper his translation with digressions and personal reflections. When he advises women to sacrifice their hair to make ballistic missiles, he adds, with a little irony, that, of course, chaste

women would prefer to see their face made ugly in this way, if it meant that they could remain free alongside their husbands, rather than keep their beauty and go over to the enemy. Regarding the cleanliness of the camps, he deplores the laziness and the lack of hygiene of the French who, "as became obvious in our time and our memory in Tunis and Aragon", relieved themselves anywhere at all and left their dead animals lying around, thus infecting the atmosphere of the camp.

Three or four years later, Jean Priorat put Jean de Meung's translation into verse. He had followed Otto IV of Burgundy on the great expedition led by Philip III the Bold against the King of Aragon. The army passed through Carcassonne where a final series of works was bringing the fortifications to their best (the

The arbalet
Here the arbalet is represented on a funeral stele found near Carcassonne. One can clearly see the stirrup, where the person using the machine could put his foot so as to be able to pull the cord with all the force of his body. At the other end, the slackening is visible.

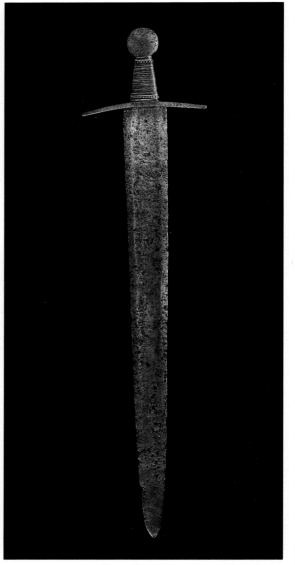

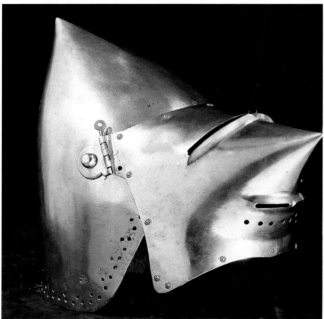

Pieces of equipment of the 12th or 13th century

A bacinet *worn over the hood of mail. A partridge beak* bacinet
(end 13th century), with the mezail *(mobile vizor) resembling a bird's beak.
A sword (end 12th or beginning 13th century), about 80 cm long, used
for cutting and thrusting. A groove going along two-thirds of the blade
made the sword lighter.*

Coat of mail, around 1350

It was for a long time believed that the word maille *(mail) came from the
Latin* macula *(staines, then meshes of a net). The etymology is more probably*
malleus *(hammer). The* mailles *are iron pieces fashioned with a hammer
and nailed on to a leather garment, or metal rings. Here, the hauberk
is of* mailles treslies, *i.e. interlaced rings.*

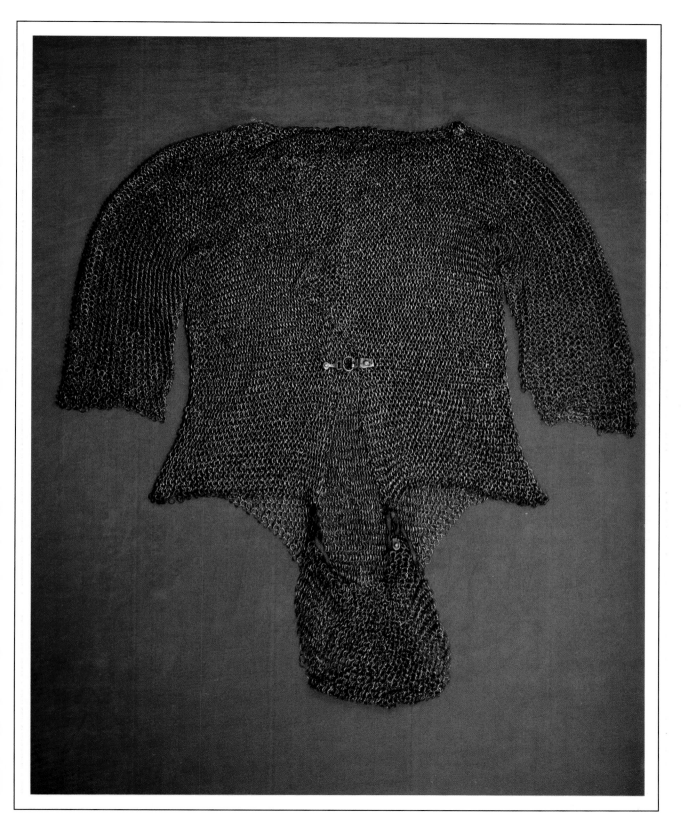

Porte
Narbonnaise,
Plan 1
Tour
du Trésau,
Plan 2

reflected and stimulated a climate of invention and innovation.

As very often in erstwhile France, innovation assumed the trappings of an idealised past. In 1147, when Geoffrey Plantaganet was given the formula for making an incendiary bomb by the monks of Noirmoutiers, he was told that it came from the writings of Vegetius. The Roman author had written no such thing, but his name was used as an august guarantee for a preparation containing most probably a concoction of grease, oil, sulphur, naphta and salpetre. The Byzantines, skilled in the art of using whatever ingredients they had to hand, were past masters at these kinds of confections.

Missile-projecting machines: mangonels, *trébuchets, pierrières*

A new kind of machine for projecting missiles appeared, but this time, apparently, it owed nothing to the devices known in Roman times. Nor do we know whether it originated in the Arab world or in Europe. These machines were pendulum-based rather than spring-operated. The main component was a long rod positioned on a pivot, with a receptacle for the missile at one end, and at the other end the cords which had to be pulled sharply. Two improvements were rapidly made to these machines. A big sling was attached to the rod, thus doubling the range of the appliance, and a counterweight fixed to the other end. It then became necessary to lower the opposite branch by means of a winch, which when released gave a far greater thrust than that produced by the ropes alone. Villard de Honnecourt describes one of these engines: ''Should you wish to construct one of these machines known as the *trébuchet* be very careful. First of all there is the platform which is placed on the ground. In front you have the two winches and the un-

construction of the Narbonne Gate and the Trésau Tower) and where certain of Vegetius' recommendations concerning defence were being applied.

These translations, these borrowings were sometimes the work of poets in the service of great lords, sometimes that of religious theoreticians of political law like Gilles of Rome who, at the same period, was responsible for the education of the future Philip le Bel, sometimes the work of practical men (architects or war leaders). But the result was never the simple observance of rediscovered rules, or the abject application of long-forgotten recipes. This taste for Vegetius or for the ''stratagems'' of Frontin (a catalogue of tricks which sometimes goes a bit far) both

Reconstruction of a catapult

This kind of engine, used by the Greeks and the Romans, could thrust stones weighing a talent (about 60 pounds). Coils of cords were used for the springs. Drawing by J.-C. Golvin, from Pour la Science, *Soedel and Foley, May 1979.*

wound rope which is used to bring back the rod as shown on the other page. The weight to be carried is substantial, since the counterweight, a bin filled with earth, is extremely heavy. It is two *toises* long [*toise* = approximately 6 feet], nine feet wide and 12 feet deep...'' For his *Étude sur le passé et l'avenir de l'artillerie,* the Prince-Président Louis-Napoléon Bonaparte had a *trébuchet* made in 1850. The rod was 32 feet long and the counterweight weighed 4 1/2 tons. When it was tried out at Vincennes ''after some tentative efforts'', it propelled a mass of 12 kilos to a distance of 175 yards. It also thrust bombs of various dimensions filled with earth to a distance of 120 to 125 yards. The machine, it would seem, shot straight, with a deviation of only 15 feet.

In fact there was a whole range of pendulum-based engines, each with its own advantage. The simplest, operated by ropes, lacked power, but had the advantage of being easy and quick to make. A fragment of a bas-relief on the wall of a south chapel in the nave of Saint-Nazaire in Carcassonne portrays a mixed system combining rope-traction and a small counterweight (we shall come back to this fragment known as the ''siege stone'', which is said to represent the death of Simon de Montfort outside Toulouse). Other machines were fitted with counterweights of several tons, making them extremely powerful. Finally, Gilles of Rome speaks of devices with mobile counterweights or double counterweights, one in a fixed position, one revolving round the rod. An abundance of words, often expressive, if not always easy to interpret, bears witness to this diversification of war engines.

The machines which gave cover to those trying to approach the walls were called *vignes,* (since these galleries bring to mind

Eglaise Saint-Nazaire, Plan 17

A mangonel

The propulsion force came from a counterweight which was lowered to the ground by means of a winch. The shooting range of the machine could be significantly increased by using a pouch (connected to the rod by cords) to extend the rod. Drawing by J.-C. Golvin, from a manuscript in Christ Church College Library, Oxford.

vineyard arbours), *tortues* (tortoises), and also *chats* or *chattes* (cats). The last word might come from the Latin *murilegus* (mouse-trap) which had been used to refer to the covered galleries, probably because they resembled those boxes or traps fitted with a spring lever and furnished with bait for catching mice. The jump is easily made from the Latin mouse-catcher to the French *chat* (cat).

Spring-based machines were mostly called scorpions, catalpults, cables, partridges or balistas (the latter might also be a reference to crossbows of varying force).

The pendulum-based machines were also called *trébuchets, trabuc, mangonneaux, martinets, couillards* (big-balled), *bricoles*... The chroniclers, who were rarely specialists, used these words rather haphazardly, or spoke quite simply of stone-throwing machines or propelling machines *(machina jaculatoria)*. The purpose of these stone-throwing machines was to demolish the wooden defence works (palisades, scaffolding, covered galleries...), the more unsound parts of the wall, or the crenellation on the façades, to smash in the rooves of the towers and

A pendulum *pierrière* (stone-throwing machine)

*On this bas-relief dating from the beginning of the 13th century,
a fairly primitive pendulum machine can be seen in action.
A soldier is about to put the stone in the sling, while others
prepare to set the rod in motion by pulling the cords.
Fragment of the siege stone, church of Saint-Nazaire.*

houses, and even the vaults of a dungeon or a castle, as at Castelnaudary in September 1211. They were sometimes used to throw "incendiary bombs", made essentially of oil, pitch or sulphur, or barrels full of refuse and the bodies of decaying animals with the aim of producing some kind of "plague".

The "ingénieurs"

In the 13th century no real siege to speak of took place without siege engines. It is true that at any one time only a few engines were used, most often one two or three. On rare occasions a maximun of ten might have been used. They took a long time to position, regulate, and load, and even the biggest could only shoot up to 20 stones a day. But, with the improvements in fortifications, they became practically indispensable for successfully attacking a strong fortress. They definitely had a significant psychological effect, and the sense of security provided by the city walls began to dwindle. Those on the defence used them to neutralise the enemy's machines, and they almost always figure in the arsenals of a fortress. It can be assumed that the producers of these machines were held in esteem (one was made a knight) and were well recompensed. They were either engaged for a whole campaign, or hired when needed. They were either experienced laymen or clerics. Peter of Vaux-de-Cernay praises the merits of William, Archdeacon of Paris, who organised collections "for the expenses of war engines", who went into the forest to choose the trees, "instructed the blacksmiths, supervised the work of the carpenters and was the superior of all the specialists".

During the third siege of Toulouse, the first thing that the besieged did was to diplay the relics of Saint Exupère and then "to order the best carpenters to set up

calabres (catapults, stone-throwing machines and other war engines) in the courtyards throughout the town, and "to ask Bernard Paraire and Master Garnier, who were skilled in such matters, to put out the *trébuchets*". In order to finish off Montsegur in 1243, the royal army appealed to the Bishop of Albi, because he knew best how to regulate and use the war engines. In the great armies like those of the King of France or the King of England, a specific corps was set up, led by a *magister ingeniorum* (master of engineers), specialised in the construction and maintenance of war engines. Rivers were used to transport that part of the equipment which followed the army during a compaign. For this reason, the great expeditions usually followed the river network. For the overland route, heavy convoys were necessary; the biggest machines were broken down into separate parts for the journey, while the smaller ones were hoisted onto carts or attached to wheels and then pulled along by oxen. A number of towns and castles were also used to store the machines. The profusion of forests in medieval France meant that a large number of machines could be made on the spot where they were needed.

And so we see that siege warfare demanded a whole panoply of logistics. Time, money, inventiveness, effective propulsion machines, determined leaders, and a sizeable army, all these were undoubtedly far more important than the splendid clash of armour, the striking sword thrusts, the lance charges, the glittering helmets and the emblazoned coats of mail, which were so much appreciated in the tournaments. The siege and defence of a town were not however a simple matter of resources and tactics. In the following studies of four sieges, an attempt will be made to understand the political, economic, social and psychological dimensions.

ASSAULTS AND SIEGES

Defence is the child of attack. It draws its *raison d'être* and its methods from past attacks and those to come. It is both a response to the enemy attack and a search for the most appropriate reaction to the enemy's manœuvres. To illustrate this dual act, which culminated at Carcassonne in the transformation of the Cité into a veritable model of military architecture, and to expose the different aspects of the struggle, four episodes will be described. These four sieges, all of great significance for the history of Carcassonne, and all sufficiently close to each other in time to be treated together, well demonstrate the panoply of resources put into operation, and the range of situations experienced.

Béziers (July 1209)

It was undoubtedly at Béziers in July 1209, rather than at Carcassonne a month later, that the fate of Raymond-Roger Trencavel was decided. As soon as he learned that the Crusaders had passed Montpellier and were about to enter his territory, the Viscount went to Béziers where he exhorted the Biterrois to defend themselves "with force and courage", after which he returned to Carcassonne; the imbalance between the Crusaders army and that on which Trencavel could count, explains the choice made by the Viscount. The knights faithful to him were too few in number to be effectively divided between the two towns of which he was the direct lord, although in the case of Béziers he shared his rights with the Bishop. It would seem that the defence of Béziers had been limited to deepening the trenches, which, as at Carcassonne, did not contain water, and to making the sides of the trenches steeper. Apart from that, the town put its trust in its position, located as it was on a fairly steep slope, and in the solidity of "the walls which completely surrounded it and kept it well closed".

The Bishop, Renaud de Montpeyroux, who had gone to parley with the Crusaders, returned with their conditions: the Catholics could either give up the heretics or leave the town so as not to perish with them; in this case their goods would not be considered as loot.

Most sieges were preceded and interrupted by attempts at negotiation. The strength of the fortifications then became an advantage for those on the defence. By giving the impression that a long immobilisation and difficult fighting lay ahead, they incited the aggressors to moderate or even forgo their demands. The reply given by the Biterrois assembled in their cathedral, as reported by William of Tudèle, gives a good idea of such reasoning. Protected by its walls, the town could hold out "for a whole month". Whereas "they were convinced that the army of the Crusaders would not stay very long. It stretched out over a league and the routes and roadways were too narrow for it". In other words, such a large army could not live off the land. The greater part of the Biterrois population had not

made "a pact with death" (Peter of Vaux-de-Cernay). It is easy to write with hindsight, but the reasoning of the Biterrois was far from ridiculous.

The problem of supplies was very often just as crucial for the besiegers as for those on the defence. In view of the slow progress of armies, the besieged almost always had the time to stock up with rations. The Crusaders covered 10 to 20 kilometres a day and arrived in a country which they barely knew, so little in fact that William of Tudèle emphasises the role of the Count of Toulouse "who always walks ahead and knows where to camp". In the absence of any kind of organisation, everyone did as best he could. In the worst of circumstances the villagers fled, taking their cereals with them, hiding them, or even destroying them. Even at the best of times, obtaining food could be very expensive, since pillaging was not systematic. Demand suddenly outstripped supply and prices soared. Peter of Vaux-de-Cernay confirms this: "The lack of any provisioning system resulted in high food prices in the camp."

The Crusaders pitched camp in front of Béziers on 22nd July 1209. At this point the Biterrois appear to have behaved very

oddly. From the first day of the siege, they showed no intention of staying behind the walls and waiting until the enemy broke ranks or gave up. A small troop came out of the town, let fly volleys of arrows and attacked isolated individuals. The skirmish acted as a provocation, not to the Crusading knights who took no notice and did not appear anxious to make an assault, but to the "mob", or in other words, the squires-in-arms. If the latter had been confronted with a *sortie* by a group of heavily armoured knights, they would probably have kept sensibly aside, but they felt themselves up to this adversary. According to William of Tudèle, they jumped down into the ditches, and armed with clubs and picks, slashed into the wall, while others started to break down the gates. Seeing that the attack was off to a good start, the Crusader knights began to put on their armour. Peter Belperron, one of the most reliable historians of the Crusade, does not believe that this attack could have succeeded "without preparation" nor that it could have been carried out by men armed in such a haphazard way. He considers, rather, that the Biterrois were surprised by the reaction of the "mob" and were not quick enough in

Town siege
*A summary of the main methods of attack with, from left to right,
a mangonel (here a barrel filled with earth is probably used for
the counterweight), escalading, sapping. Engraving from a manuscript
of the Bibliothèque de l'Arsenal, 13th century.*

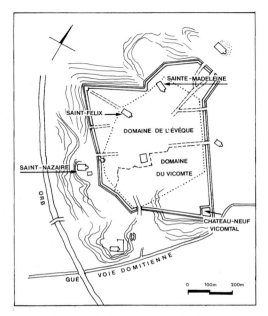

assault, they quickly put down the ladders, and the town is taken''. Quite clearly, there were few people ''accustomed to the hardships of war'' at Béziers. Overwhelming as it was, the taking of Béziers did not follow the usual rules of siege warfare. It was a good warning against those model scenarios which present the siege as an unchanging ritual; it demonstrated that in siege warfare the role played by chance, by blunders, by gross tactical errors and panic reactions should never be overlooked.

The mob who had taken the initiative in the assault, did not stop at slaughtering everybody who crossed their path. They carried out a shocking massacre in the cathedral. Then they entered the houses and took away anything of value, and in this way made themselves masters of fabulous spoils.

Although they do not seem to have done much to stop the massacre, the Crusader knights reacted promptly to the looting. The mob was thrown outside ''as though they were dogs''. Now that they had become poor again just as fast as they had become rich, ''these ne're-do-wells took justice into their hands for the spoliation they considered they had suffered, and set fire to the town and its treasures. There was a quick return to the camp''.

The results of this first important siege of the Crusade were not particularly brilliant: a considerable booty had gone up in smoke, a great number of women and children had been slaughtered, the blood of heretics had been mixed with that of good Catholics, a church had been the scene of the very worst acts of carnage, a major part of the town had been destroyed by fire. There had been no place for the chivalric ideal nor had the siege been of great interest to the knights. In this blind and savage hecatomb we see little trace of the objectives fixed by Innocent III for the Crusades.

returning to their town. With the enemy on their heels, they crowded in through the gates, but were not able to close them in time. All resistance on the part of the population immediately collapsed. It was as though the psychological tension had been too much. ''Then they knew from the bottom of their heart that they would not be able to hold out, and they took refuge in the cathedral'' (William of Tudèle). It is tempting to compare this passage with chapter XII of *Military Institutions* by Vegetius. The Roman author was well aware that in normal circumstances ''attack is more costly in human terms than defence'', but, he adds ''the besieged are more frightened..., if they are not used to danger and are surprised by the first

Béziers in 1209

According to the report sent by the legates to Innocent III, the town ''appeared to be so well defended by nature, by men and by the supplies in the town, that is seemed that it could withstand the siege of any army for a long time''. Drawing by J.-C. Golvin, taken from l'Histoire du Languedoc, P. Wolff (ed.), Privat, 1967.

The Crusaders decided to use this senseless massacre as a recipe for winning future sieges. "All and everyone of them agreed that whenever the army came before a fortified town and where that town refused to surrender, the inhabitants would be slaughtered once the town had been taken. They were sure that after such examples, the terror would be so great that no town would dare offer resistance." The taking of the town in less than a day was no longer seen as a piece of luck, but as a demonstration of an overwhelming force. The credibility of threats, an essential element in all strategy, had been amply demonstrated. According to the letter of the legates Milon and Arnaud Amaury, a hundred castles and fortified villages between Béziers and Carcassonne surrendered to the Crusaders without resistance, or were found abandoned. After lingering for three days on the banks of the Orb, the army reached Carcassonne in less than a week, without striking a blow.

Carcassonne (August 1209)

Trencavel decided to defeat the Crusaders' army at Carcassonne. "He assembled there the greatest possible number of knights", says Peter of Vaux-de-Cernay. The Cité was well protected by a wall 15 to 22 feet high and an average of 9 feet wide, with about 30 towers spaced at intervals of 60 to 90 feet. It was admittedly an ancient fortification, dating probably from the Later Empire, but much

Montségur
The Béziers massacre was the beginning of a reign of terror which only ended in 1244 at Montségur.

more solid and better flanked than many of the city defences of the time. Where the towns had any defences at all, the walls were usually not so thick and there were far fewer towers.

The two bourgs to the north and south of the Cité, and which communicated with it through the gates of the Gallo-Roman wall, were not so well defended. As Peter of Vaux-de-Cernay says, ''each was provided with walls and trenches''. The bourgs were as populated as the Cité. So the Cité was not the isolated citadel we see today, but rather the acropolis of a vast agglomeration with an ill-defined perimeter and fairly mediocre defences. The strategy to be adopted seemed simple: first defend the bourgs, and if they fell, take refuge in the Cité.

This staggering of the defence was less obvious than might appear, since the strongest part of the defence system, the Cité, was the worst supplied with water. The sandstone of the mound on which the town was built, was extremely porous, but there were a few clay deposits at varying depths where the water which filtered through gathered, forming natural cisterns.

There were wells to reach these water pockets, but they depended on the amount and the frequency of the rain falling on the mound itself. The inhabitants drew their water mainly from the Font-grande spring, situated lower down on the hillside occupied by the south bourg, and at the far bigger supply basin. It was also **L'Aude,** possible to go down to the Aude, where **Plan 23** the animals could drink, and where the inhabitants could fill their leather water bottles. The way down was short, not much more than 500 yards, but the climb back to the Aude Gate (or its equivalent at that time), was hard-going. The location of the main water points outside the city walls, was one of the causes of the Crusaders' success.

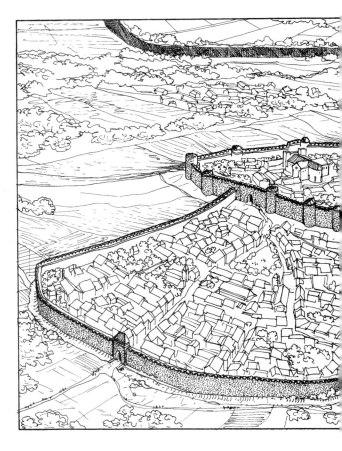

''No later than the day after they arrived, our men, counting on taking the first bourg by assault, [most certainly the bourg of Saint-Michel to the south which was not so well fortified as the other], rushed towards it together, without even bothering to use the siege engines'' (Peter of Vaux-de-Cernay).

The knights did not like this kind of unprepared assault. They felt that it involved a lot of risks, with little guarantee of success. It meant jumping down into the trenches armed with ladders wide enough for men to climb up two or three abreast, then setting the ladders against the wall, then climbing up with a few

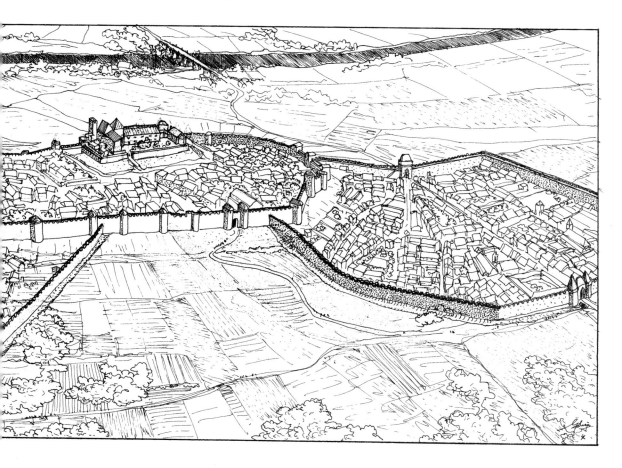

companions, or rather trying to pull one self up to the crenellated parapet and climbing over, then exposing oneself to the arrows and rocks thrown down from the neighbouring towers, all the time battling against a deluge of stones. Moreover the ladders often fell down as they were pushed away from the wall by the defenders with long wooden forks. In this case, the attackers could either drop down themselves or engage in an unequal combat if they actually managed to keep a foothold. Surprise attacks involved all these risks, yet there was usually little hope of succeeding. The enemy, however, was quickly outnumbered and they retreated, abandonning the town. The town was immediately destroyed and the trenches filled in, since it was understandably feared that the town might be retaken. The next day, an attempt to conquer the second bourg in the same way met with defeat. Peter of Vaux-de-Cernay continues: "In this battle, one of our

The Cité and its bourgs in 1209

An approximate reconstruction of the urban agglomeration of Carcassonne. In the south (on the left) the bourg of Saint-Michel, in the north (on the right) the bourg of Saint-Vincent, crossed by the old Roman road. The Cité is surrounded by the Later Empire wall. Drawing by J.-C. Golvin.

knights was wounded in the thigh and was trapped in the ditch; nobody dared go back to help him out because of the stones which continued to fall. But one brave man, the Count of Montfort, jumped down into the ditch, accompanied only by his squire, and saved the injured man while putting his own life to risk.'' Montfort had already distinguished himself in the previous assault: ''The first of them all, indeed the only one of all the knights, he dared to throw himself into the trench and contributed more than any other to the taking of the town.''

This description of Montfort's bravery prepares the reader for the barons' subsequent choice of a minor lord from the outskirts of the Ile-de-France as the new Viscount of Carcassonne and Béziers. These feats of arms and the manner in which they are described also throw light on what Georges Duby calls ''the central values of the knightly ethic[8]''. The following is taken largely from Duby.

In the previous century, courage had been considered a passive virtue, consisting of waiting patiently. Danger was accepted, but one did not go looking for it. A hundred years later, at the time of Bouvines and of the Crusade, courage had become a vehicle for action. A good knight had to be valiant, that is he had to accomplish feats of valour. ''Temerity had upstaged prudence'', writes Georges Duby. Peter of Vaux-de-Vernay wanted to enhance the reputation of Montfort and he gave many examples of bravery of the ''noble Count''. Peter of Vaux-de-Cernay, who is often allusive and easily gives in to the temptation of biblical reference, loses no opportunity here for going into concrete details, and this lends a certain truth to his examples.

In siege warfare, courage is not enough. To get into the second bourg, the Crusaders had to resort to siege engines, as was the custom. The episode, as related by Peter of Vaux-de-Cernay, is a model of its kind. The Crusaders began by preparing a battery of missile-hurling machines, and targetting them in the direction of the wall, in particular at the battlement parapet and the sentry-route. Few of these siege machines were powerful enough to bring down part of a thick wall, even when the missiles directly struck their target with great force. But it was always possible to breach the top of the curtain and in this way prevent the defenders from occupying it. Once this was done the sappers took over. They went down into the ditches as best as they could, taking ''a four-wheeled cart covered with ox hides to shelter the specialists as they mined the wall''. ''The enemy threw down a continual stream of firebrands [most probably lighted faggots], wood [logs or broken beams], and stones, and soon destroyed the cart. But the sappers took refuge in the niche they had already dug, and in this way they were able to carry on with their work without any interruption''. Sapping was more time-consuming but easier than mining; both techniques had the same objective, that of causing a wall to collapse by depriving it of its base. Sapping consisted of digging a fairly wide, deep hole in the wall. At the same time, according to Jean de Meung the sappers ''propped up and supported'' the wall, which they scooped out with the driest rafters they could find, to prevent it from collapsing (trebuchier). This technique was known in Paris as ''estagier'' or propping up. Following this, straw and wood were placed around the bottom of the props which the sappers then ignited, before leaving. When the wooden structure supporting the wall was consumed by the fire, the wall itself collapsed. This was exactly what happened at daybreak and ''our men rushed through the breach with a great din'', writes Peter of Vaux-de-Cernay. The besieged took

The Cité seen from the banks of the River Aude
It was here, apparently, "beside the water", that the Crusaders pitched their camp.

refuge in the Cité, then sallied out again, because the Crusaders thought that they had won the battle and had gone back to their camps. A few dawdlers, who were probably busy accumulating loot, were struck down. The Carcassonians set light to the bourg and locked themselves up in their Cité.

In overcoming the resistance of the two bourgs, the Crusaders had not achieved anything spectacular. Trencavel does not seem to have deployed all his forces on these first lines of defence. However, this first week of battle (from 1st to 8th August) was full of omen. The Cité was now packed, not only with the normal inhabitants and peasants from the surrounding countryside who had decided to take refuge there on hearing of the arrival of the Crusaders, but also, and most significantly, with the entire populations of the two bourgs. When the besieged abandonned the south bourg, they lost control of the Fontgrande spring and the Aude. According to William of Tudèle, the Crusaders were able to get round the enemy positions lying between them and the river, as early as the first attack. They then denied the Carcassonians access to the water. The Count of Toulouse even had his tent set up "in a meadow by the side of the water". It was there, surrounded by his chief barons that he received the King of Aragon, who had come as mediator. The intervention of Peter II of Aragon was in keeping with the duty of aid and council which a lord and his vassal owed each other. Hostilities were interrupted, the King entered the Cité, escorted by three companions. The speech which William of Tudèle accredits to the King of Aragon, is a kind of review and analysis of the situation. By referring to the massacre of Béziers, and the exactions of the Crusaders on his territory, Raymond-Roger posed as a victim, entitled to the aid of his suzerain. But Peter

L'Aude, Plan 23

II refused to be drawn into this trap. He had, on several occasions, instructed Trencavel to chase out the heretics, and if the Viscount was now experiencing "torments and anguish", it was because of these "mad people". When Trencavel saw the King and the army he had brought with him, he had had a fleeting moment of hope that his lord would give him military support. But it was not to be. In view of the unequal numbers, the possibility of a "shield and lance" battle on open ground between the Trencavel's knights and the Crusader knights, was more or less out of the question. Finally, if the town was well fortified, it was also overcrowded, packed with women and children. It was time to parley. Trencavel left that to the King of Aragon. The French put the bar very high: the Viscount could leave the town with twelve of his men. As for the rest of the population, they would be at the mercy of the Crusaders. This is what in today's language would be termed total capitulation. Moreover, the example of the Béziers massacre gave the besieged no reason to expert any kind of generosity from the Crusaders.

Peter II considered the terms inacceptable, but he communicated them to the Viscount and then left for Aragon. The Viscount refused the terms of surrender, considering that it would be dishonourable to abandon his subjects.

It was then that the real siege of the Cité began. "The Crusaders gathered together what was necessary to fill the ditches, they cut down branches and made *chats* and *chattes*. The army chiefs spent the whole day riding round to determine the best place from where they might surprise the besieged" (William of Tudèle). In those days it was impossible to guard the whole of the city defences in a uniform way. The Cité walls for example were approximately one kilometre in perimeter. A small group of besiegers only had to at-

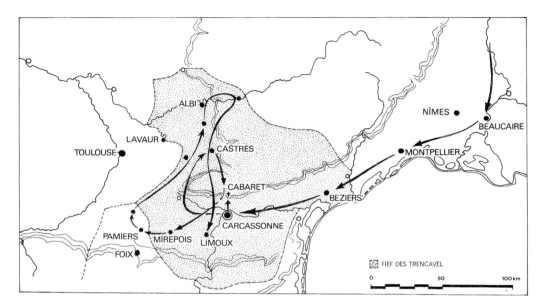

tack one point of the wall with a great show of force and noise and most of the defenders would rush to the danger spot, leaving the rest of the wall insufficiently protected to resist a solid attack.

If the Crusaders were busy, so were the people of Carcassonne. "The Viscount and his men climbed up onto the wall and the shots from the crossbow left dead in various parts" (William of Tudèle). It is possible that this feverish activity was what is called "gesticulation" in today's language of strategy, in other words a show of force which the opponent is expected to interpret. In this case, it would seem that both sides wished to demonstrate their determination. However, by the 15th August, the Crusaders were masters of the

Cité, Trencavel had been imprisoned, and the population was safe and sound but had been forced to leave the Cité leaving all their possessions behind.

The siege came to a quick end for various reasons. The first is that both Trencavel and the Crusaders were trapped by the time factor. The Viscount knew that he would not be able to last out for a long time in an overcrowded city with no water supply. William of Tudèle emphasises this point: "Even if there had not been so many refugees from the surrounding countryside crowded into the citadel, and even if the Crusaders had waited as long as a year, they would not have been able to take the town by assault, for the towers were so high and the walls so crenel-

The 1209 Campaign

In spite of the victories at Béziers and Carcassonne, the taking of Mirepoix, the absence of any resistance in Limoux, and the allegiance of the clergy at Pamiers and Albi, the Trencavel fief had not by any means been entirely subjected by the end of 1209. Although the Duke of Burgundy gave his support, the attack against Cabaret did not succeed. Drawing by J.-C. Golvin, from l'Histoire du Languedoc, P. Wolff (ed.), Privat, Toulouse, 1967.

lated." But the Crusaders controlled the water points and the wells had dried up, for it was the middle of summer and the heat was extreme. He goes on to list the other problems, the cries of the women and children, the flies, and sickness. In addition, a great number of livestock had been slaughtered and skinned to provide fresh hides for the protection of the wooden engines from fire, and this had produced a terrible stench throughout the Cité. The picture is perhaps a little overdone; William of Tudèle, never a good poet at the best of times, never hesitates before a cliché and exagerates the torments of the besieged "who had never suffered so much since they were born". One thing was sure: the situation could only get worse and time was not on Trencavel's side. Nor for that matter on the side of the Crusaders. They had set out at the beginning of July, and many had no intention of going beyond the obligatory 40 days feudal service. Those who continued would have to be paid. The legates leading the Crusade and the great lords who had brought their vassals with them, knew that they could not afford to let the expedition drag on if they did not want to see the army melt away. In short, everybody started thinking about the outcome of the conflict. The objective behind the conflict was a subject of reflection. The aim of the Crusade was not to occasion death and desolation, but to fight Catharism and to replace a viscount who had shown himself incapable of combating heresy, with a true follower of the Faith. The reasoning of the Crusaders as exposed by Peter of Vaux-de-Cernay is henceforth perfectly logical.

"The Crusaders held council to decide how to take possession of the town. If events were to go as they had at Béziers, the town would be destroyed and everything it contained lost. In this case, the person who was to become the new count would have no resources with which to pay the knights and sergeants needed for the defence of the fief."

The Béziers tragedy must have weighted even heavier in Trencavel's decision. If he decided to resist, he would expose his subjects to probable slaughter, should the enemy attack succeed, or to a slow death, should the siege continue. The young Count preferred to sacrifice himself. On 15th August "a powerful lord" approached the Cité. His mission was to convince the Viscount that the time had come to negotiate. The Viscount, escorted by a good number of his men, went out to meet him and followed him to the Crusaders' camp. Raymond-Roger, surrounded by his closest vassals, listened as the barons dictated their terms. Peter of Vaux-de-Cernay summarises them as follows: "The inhabitants would have to leave the town with nothing on them, Trencavel would be imprisoned and a new viscount chosen". The people of Carcassonne did in effect leave "in their shirts and breeches with no other clothes". Some went to Toulouse, others to Aragon... There was of course no question of expelling them indefinitely, for the new viscount could not rule over a deserted town. But this was a way of both severely punishing the population, and rewarding the Crusaders, without running the risk of throwing the victor and vanquished together, and thus creating a dangerous breeding ground of mutual hatred, with exactions coming from one side and rebelious resentment from the other. In brief, as a result of this kind of "look out", the return of any Carcassonians, who wished to go back to their homes once the feudal army broke up, could be interpreted as an act of allegiance to the new lord.

It now remained to choose the new seigneur. Most of the great barons considered that the expedition was over and almost all were eager to return to their domains.

The Crusaders had started to accumulate loot and to share it out, but the legate Arnaud Amaury, Abbot of Cîteaux, promptly assembled them and ordered them, under pain of excommunication, not to take anything from the town. Everything had to be returned to the future lord of the country. To make doubly sure, a number of knights were nominated to guard the loot. These guards quickly helped themselves to 50,000 livres. If this figure is exact (and it most surely is, for it is quoted in a letter by Innocent II, and the Pope's Exchequer was not in the habit of trifling with such matters), it was a nice little sum. The election of Simon de Montfort was probably the work of Arnaud Amaury, the very influential papal legate, who was more than just the spiritual leader of the Crusade. The choice was a good one: a lord who was neither too powerful, nor too obscure, but honest, a sincere believer, respectful and obedient in his relations with the Holy See, and held in esteem by

The Cité fortifications in 1209

It should have been possible to defend the Cité without any problem,
since the Later Empire wall was still solid and there were many
towers spaced out at regular intervals along the wall.
On the left, we see the North Gate,
which communicated with the bourg of Saint-Vincent.
It was probably walled up after the loss of the bourg.

Philip Augustus, who would not feel threatened by this surprising promotion.

By the end of August, most of the Crusaders' army had dispersed. William of Tudèle speaks of the new Viscount as ''in great difficulty and in pensive mood, for very few of his companions had agreed to stay with him. As for Raymond-Roger Trencavel, he languished as a prisoner in his own residence, or, according to Peter of Vaux-de-Cernay, ''in a castle near Carcassonne''. He died on 10th November 1209 from a bout of dysentry, poisoned, some said, for he was a young man and had died suddenly. But these doubts were dismissed by the chroniclers.

What can be deduced from this second episode? From 1st August to 8th August, the successful attacks against the two bourgs flanking the Cité well reflect the moderate effort needed to take settlements which were only fairly well fortified. In the course of the next week, factors other than those of arms were to determine the fate of the Cité itself, which was well protected by its walls. The isolation and fear of the besieged, who could not count on the help of any ally and feared another massacre, the time issue, problematic for both sides, and political decisions, practical on the Crusaders' side, generous on the part of Raymond-Roger. The surrender of the Viscount, the saving of the population, including the heretics, the confiscation of the Trencavel lands and their transfer to Montfort, are the outcomes of this period, during which each side had calculated its chances of winning, had envisaged certain results, estimated the eventual gains or losses. And this is the way things happen in certain sieges, just as in chess: after a period of reflection, each side admits that it would be pointless to carry on since a draw or a checkmate are inevitable.

Toulouse
(October 1217 - July 1218)

The obstination and the determination of both sides are the key factors of this siege. On the one hand there was the town: most of the fortifications had been raised, the population had had its arms confiscated, the count was a fickle, changeable man, who was not interested in warfare. On the other side we have a leader who was short of money, men and time, and whose luck seems to have run out. One would expect the outcome to have been one of those that often occurred in medieval wars, ie where appearances were saved but nothing resolved. But in fact, no negotiations were to be opened either before or during the siege. The death of Simon de Montfort on 25th June 1218 and the discouragement of his son brought the confrontation to an end.

A combination of Raymond VI's unwillingness to oppose the heretics, the intransigence of the legates, and Montfort's own ambition, had led the latter to attack the Count of Toulouse. By 1212 Montfort was in control of most of Raymond VI's lands. In 1214, the troops of Raymond VI, together with those of the King of Aragon, who had come to his aid, were crushed at Muret. After hesitating for some time, Innocent II confirmed the confiscation of Raymond VI's lands at the Lateran Council (November 1215), but left the lands he had beyond the Rhône to the Count's son, on condition that ''by certain signs, he shows himself worthy of mercy''. Even before this decision and without obtaining the consent of the pope, Simon had sent his brother Guy to take possession of Toulouse. Guy set himself up in the Narbonnais Castle, a fortress at the south entrance of the town, and ordered the inhabitants to destroy the town walls immediately. ''They obeyed against their will with many complaints'' (Peter of Vaux-de-Cernay).

Simon did not like this town, swarming as it was with heretics (or so he thought) and money-lenders. He felt that it had ''too much of a shopkeeper's mentality'', that is was too rich and too ''democratic'' with its elected consuls who dispensed justice, administered the town, controlled an armed force, and signed treaties without the intervention of the seigneur. In 1216, Montfort had to abandon Beaucaire to put down the population of Toulouse which was preparing to welcome Raymond VI. After some street fighting, negotiations were opened. The result was that the knights and the many burgesses who served in the town's militia were forced to give up their arms, a number of hostages were taken from the elite of the population and sent to be held in various castles, and all buildings and constructions which might help in the defence of the city were pulled down.

On 13th September, Raymond VI once again entered Toulouse to the cheers of an enthusiastic population, who ''kissed his clothes'' and ''shed tears of joy''. Montfort heard of this while he was fighting in Provence. There were not enough Frenches in the town to put up any significant resistance to what was happening. The people of Toulouse began to fortify their town, ''surrounding it with a great number of barricades and ditches'' (Peter of Vaux-de-Cernay). ''So many rich workmen had never been seen before; everybody took part in the work: the Count and all the knights, the burgesses and their wives, worthy merchants, men and women and money-lenders, boys and girls, servants and messengers, all carrying pikes, spades and simple pitchforks. Everybody put their heart and soul into the work.'' This unanimity on the part of the population, which the Song praises and which was later given expression on

Simon de Montfort's seal

Hunting was also a way of training for warfare. On the other side there is a lion with a forked tail, like that on the Montfort arms: De gueules au lion d'argent la queue, fourchée et passée en sautoir.

the battlefield, is the main reason for the success of the Toulouse resistance. The defence was perfectly organised. The "gallant men", armed with lances and stones, were positioned on the barricades; others were stationed below on the mound with lances and boar-spears to defend the lists and stop the enemy from reaching the palisades. The archers and crossbowmen took up position at the loopholes. Beside them they had vats (wooden tubs used in the grape harvest) full of arrows and quarrels. Behind were the "ladies and the women", who fetched the rocks and stones, and everywhere there were people armed with anything they could get hold of, axes, sledge-hammers...

This "defence" was not a withdrawal, or a test of endurance. The population was not avoiding combat; on the contrary they were preparing for it. The hastily constructed fortifications were not there as a protection against attack, but to help in the fight of this "furious and aggressive population" (combatens, in old Provençal). Montfort and his barons held council and took two decisions. The first was an obvious deduction: Toulouse was not really under siege. Supplies and reinforcements from Gascony were reaching the town via the outlying district of Saint-Cyprien situated on the left bank of the Garonne and linked to the town by two well-defended bridges. The Crusaders decided to position themselves on both sides of the river and, as the saying, goes "make two sieges". The second decision was to create a new town. This *Nova Tholosa*, set up to the south of the Narbonnais Castle, was surrounded by palisades and ditches. Immunity was granted to anybody prepared to settle there.

These two initiatives ended in failure. The "new Toulouse" never rivalled the real town. As for the blockade of the Saint-Cyprien district, it had to be lifted, because, says the Song, of a sortie on the part of the besieged. As Peter of Vaux-de-Cernay says, this double action resulted in "two weak armies". In Toulouse a council was held in the church named "little Saint-Sernin". Raymond VI assembled his principal vassals, and "the most important and the best inhabitants of the town" and the consuls. They decided to go and "rent knights", whose salary and maintenance would be paid for by the consuls. Meanwhile, new works were undertaken, "inside and outside a crowd of workers fortified the town, the gates, the bailey, the walls, the bratices, the barricades, the trenches, the lists, the bridges, the staircases..." It seems that the first line of defence (archers and stone throwers) dug themselves into the look-out turrets and behind the palisades, on the open ground behind the trenches, to stop the enemy from approaching the walls which were probably not very strong. *Trébuchets* were made and aimed in the direction of the Narbonnais Castle. A number of attacks were carried out in vain. Gui de Levis suggested they make a surprise attack at dawn since "the winter was bitter, hard, icy and dark, the men of the town would be in their beds with their wives". The fighting took place on both sides of a trench filled with icy water. The Crusaders managed to cross it, but then they were forced to retreat. It was not the fortifications which gave victory to Toulouse, but the actions and the enthusiasm of the population. Simon concluded that unless substantial reinforcements arrived "in the season of new life", any other attempts would be of no avail. "Many days passed without an attack and then Easter arrived." It was then the turn of Toulouse to take the initiative. A few knights swooped down towards the Crusaders' camp. Montfort called his troops together and counter-attacked, the aggressors fled, then made an about turn with the support of all the population

The siege of Toulouse
In this engraving, Jean-Paul Laurens (1838-1921),
from the Haute-Garonne, portrays the spirit of resistance shown
by the whole population of Toulouse.
Hôtel de Ville, Toulouse.

knights, squires, burgesses, and ordinary folk'' (ie members of the populace). After a bloody battle, each side regained its position. In May, the long-awaited reinforcements arrived. Toulouse reacted by intensifying the fortification works. The Crusaders tried unsucessfully to take the Saint-Cyprien district, Then one of those miracles happened, that Peter of Vaux-de-Cernay delighted in recounting. Three days of torrential rain reduced the trenches to slosh ''which our men, mounted on their iron-shod horses could not cross'' (Peter of Vaux-de-Cernay), and caused the palisades to subside. And then the swollen Garonne broke the two bridges in half, preventing the transport of supplies to Toulouse. Montfort and his men were able to occupy the bourg without any problem, and positioned themselves on the banks of the river.

After nine months of siege, the Count's discouragement reached its lowest point. According to William of Puylaurens, the Cardinal-legate, Bertrand, referred to Montfort as incompetent *(ignarus)* and soft *(remissus)*, which might be translated as ''wound down''. But what could he do, now that the mercenaries he was no longer able to pay were leaving one by one. When men disappoint you, a new arm can restore hope. Montfort decided to build a *chatte*, which, in the words of William of Puylaurens, would be ''so powerful that its like had never been seen since Solomon's time… and which will contain 400 of the best knights and 150 archers''. It was a wooden engine for transporting earth and other materials to fill the trenches. Once filled, the ditches could easily be crossed on foot and then it would be possible for the men to engage in close combat, break down the palisades, and jump down into the town. This enormous gallery supported by iron tenons was pushed along with ''cries and whistles''. It advanced ''with little jumps''. The

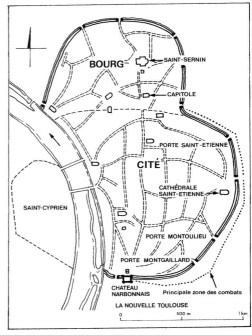

Toulouse defenders struck it with a big rock thrown down by a *trébuchet*. The *chatte* made ''a few small steps'' to position itself outside the range of the *trébuchet*. The men working the *trébuchet* adjusted their aim and again struck the *chatte*, this time breaking its madriers, killing some of the drivers and putting the others to flight. Some of the Toulouse defenders were not concerned about this *chatte* nor about another engine, a ''rolling castle (undoubtedly an attack tower), which we shall destroy all the more easily the nearer it comes'', but the majority were worried and reinforced the walls. Once again, the *chatte* moved forward

Toulouse at the time of the siege (1217-1218)
The town was too big and too well supplied via the downstream of the Aude to be completely and efficiently besieged. Drawing by J.-C. Golvin, from Heresy, Crusade and Inquisition in Southern France 1100-1250, *W.-L. Wakefield, London.*

"skilfully and rapidly", and this time the trébuchet stones damaged it a little. "In God's name, my treacherous Lady Cat *(Dame Chatte)*, you will never catch the rats", cried the defenders. On their side, the Crusaders began to doubt the tactical value of an engine which only served as a target for the enemy.

One of the consuls at Toulouse, Master Bernard, informed the knights that "the people of the bourg and the Cité have decided to make a sortie in order to destroy the *chatte* and the other engines, which, at least in the minds of the ordinary folk, who are frightened by the size of the engine, have become too dangerous a menace". It was indeed a strange siege, in which the people decided on military policy and the barons simply approved. On the morning of the 25th June, the Toulouse offensive surprised those guarding the engines, and heavy losses were sustained. Meanwhile, the other Crusaders "were still sleeping or attending Mass". Montfort was alerted and put on his armour, but did not wish to leave for battle before hearing mass. However, "as soon as he had seen his Saviour", that is immediately after the Host was raised, he rushed into the mêlée. He was hit "by a hail of stones and a shower of arrows". His brother Guy was seriously wounded in the side by an arbalet quarrel. Simon continued to defend the machines "near the trench". It was there that he died.

A carpenter of Toulouse had built a stone-throwing machine, and this engine had been dragged from Saint-Sernin, on a platform manoeuvered by ladies, young girls and married women. The stone went exactly to its target, guided probably by fate, for it could not be said that a *trébuchet* aimed with sufficient precision to hit the Count "on his steel helmet".

It is thought by some that this episode is portrayed in the bas-relief fragment called the "siege stone", to be seen in the

Saint-Nazaire Church of Carcassonne. The work is very worn, awkwardly carved and very confused. As far as one can see, the clothes of the fighters correspond to those worn at the beginning of the 13th century. A twisted relief in the centre might represent the Garonne. On the left a group of soldiers roughly lined up on three levels seems to be going into battle. On the bottom right there is a *trébuchet:* a servant is placing a stone in the pocket of the sling and at the other end of the rod a small counterweight ends in some cords, which some people (some of whom are bearded and therefore not women) are about to pull sharply. Above there is a crenellation framed by two towers which looks more like the Narbonnais Castle than the walls of Toulouse. We notice some faces on the battlements, two armed men in front of the tower, a crossbowman on the other. Above this there is a man lying down, with what looks like a sword

Eglise Saint-Nazaire, Plan 17

Raymond VI's seal

A complex personality, he alternately took the Cross and defended the heretics. After being completely dispossessed by Montfort, he set about regaining his lands in 1217, and had practically succeeded in this by the time he died in 1222. On the seal, we see the cross of Toulouse.

in his side. Another person is trying either to withdraw the sword or push it further in. Higher up an angel is taking a small child up to heaven in its arms. This is the traditional way of representing the soul of a dead man leaving this world for eternal life.

This bas-relief is interesting for the image it gives of a *trébuchet* about to be put into action, but it is less convincing as a "memorial" of the 25th June 1218. The image it projects is, in any case, sufficiently vague for everybody to interpret it as they wish.

Amaury de Montfort was not quite twenty when he succeeded his father with the consent of the barons and the benediction of the legate. Unless he was to lose honour, he could not immediately raise the siege. On Sunday 1st July, a new attempt to take the town resulted in failure. The fighting lasted all day and was so violent that both sides were exhausted. In the following days neither side attacked nor tried to win. At this point the barons and the prelates held council. A number of factors spoke for abandoning the siege, the lack of resources, the announced departure of several knights who had completed their 40 days service, the news of rebellion throughout Languedoc on the part of small lords who had heard of Simon's death. Amaury resigned himself to it. He left Carcassonne, taking his father's remains with him. The body had been boiled a long time to separate the flesh from the bones, as was the custom at that time. The flesh and the entrails were burned as soon as possible (in an unknown place), and only the bones were taken to be placed in the church of Saint-Nazaire in the Cité. A funeral stone, discovered in 1845 and today hanging against the wall of the south arm of the transept is perhaps the one which covered Montfort's coffin. The figure carved into the pink marble is wearing a coat of arms decorated with lions and the cross of Toulouse. Simon alone could combine these two emblems: his own arms (a lion with a forked tail) and the Toulouse cross. Some however question the authenticity of this stone. It seems to be hardly worn and it is true that it did not stay in place very long. In 1224, when Amaury left Carcassonne he had his father's remains disinterred. It was the only thing of value he took back with him to the Ile-de-France.

The taking of a town is not simply a matter of skilful tactics and courage; Simon de Montfort was not lacking in either. It is true that he was often in want of money to pay his men, of supplies and of equipment, and that his army expanded and shrunk with the changes in the 40 days service. But these were not insurmountable obstacles.

The fortifications he was up against were not particularly impressive; they were mostly improvised and hastily put up, in some cases they hardly existed, as for example in the Montoulieu area where the fighting took place in the open, in the gardens, vineyards and orchards. It was the people of Toulouse who defeated Simon. First because they were in good physical shape. In spite of his determination, Montfort never managed to blockade the town. The people of Toulouse received everything they needed via the Garonne and the nord-east: "What they consume each day in the way of corn, wheat, and meat keeps them in a happy, belligerent mood." Secondly, because they were ferociously determined. The rancour against "the French" turned into hatred, as can be seen from the fate reserved for their prisoners whom they cut into pieces and used as *trébuchet* fodder to be shot into the Crusaders' camp. This siege was above all a conflict of two wills, that of the Toulouse people on the one hand, who became more determined with each day that passed, on the other hand, that of Mont-

fort, whose political sense and military judgement seem to have given place to obstinate pride. As Simon says in the Song of the Crusade, "Either this town will kill me, or I shall kill the town".

Montfort's death had important consequences for Carcassonne. "When he fell, everything went to pieces, when he passed away, everything died with him", wrote Peter of Vaux-de-Cernay. Another siege at Toulouse (16th June-1st August) failed in spite of the presence of Prince Louis (the future Louis VII), who had come to complete his 40 days feudal service. From then onwards Amaury de Montfort was on the defence. The death of Raymond VI, "the old Count", only spurred on his son all the more in his attempt at reconquest. Soon Amaury had nothing more than Carcassonne and a few scattered castles. He was penniless. In January 1224, shut up in Carcassonne, he made a treaty with Raymond VII, then left the Cité with his men for the Ile-de-France. The young Raymond Trencavel, son of the dispossessed Viscount, who had been looked after by Roger Bernard de Foix, had himself proclaimed "Viscount of Béziers, Carcassonne, Razès and Albi", at the age of seventeen. It was a short-lived victory. When a new Crusading army led by King Louis VIII arrived in 1226, the people of Carcassonne, like those of all the towns of Bas-Languedoc, were very impressed, handed over the keys of the Cité. The viscounty was annexed to the royal

The Siege Stone (fragment)
This bas-relief is generally considered to be a portrayal of the death of Montfort. The child being born up by an angel in the top right represents Simon's soul.

domains and Carcassonne became the chief town of the seneschalsy. The Trencavels, like the Montforts, were feudal lords of medium ability. The town's fate was intimately linked with that of its lords. Simon's death at Toulouse sounded the death knell of the local lords. Eight years later, the town would have another master and another destiny.

Carcassonne (8th September - 11th October 1240)

On the evening of Thursday 11th October, Raymond Trencavel, the son of the dispossessed Viscount, raised the siege he had been waging against Carcassonne. After a month of violent combat and many attempts to get into the town, he gave up

The death of Simon de Montfort

Considered avid, cruel and brutal by some, a sincere believer, efficient and brave by others, this minor seigneur from the Ile-de-France has become a well-known historical figure. Engraving by E. Bayard, from G. Burgun.

the idea of taking the Cité which had been vigorously defended (in the name of the king) by the Seneschal, William of Ormes, Two days later the seneschal wrote an account of the attacks undergone and what had been done to repel them, for Blanche of Castille. This account is a godsend for the historian. Nothing can compare with this text written just after the events. It is free of poetic exageration and distant, second-hand memories, embellished with the passing of time.

Raymond Trencavel, who for a short time between 1224 and 1226 had been viscount, had gone to Aragon. From there he planned the reconquest of his lands. In the height of the summer of 1240, he crossed the Pyrénées, and was welcomed by numerous lords of the Corbières, whose submission to the king had been extremely superficial. Several towns in the region of Terménès, Razès and then of the Black Moutains, opened their gates to the Viscount and joined the rebels. They had their reasons. There was a hateful climate in the region, kept up by over-zealous inquisitors, and the petty annoyances and exorbitant demands of a royal administration which mostly lived off the country by increasing taxes and multiplying fines. Moreover, the disposessed *(faidits)* feudal lords still felt very resentful towards the new nobility from the North... However, there was no real popular uprising, it was more a movement of sympathy, a measured adhesion. Trencavel rallied a large number of Languedoc knights, but was not able to assemble an army of any considerable size. Nor did he manage to find any powerful ally. The King of Aragon did not interfere and Raymond VII, the Count of Toulouse, refused to help William of Ormes crush the rebellion, but on the other hand did nothing to positively help the Viscount and his men.

The chronicle of William of Puylaurens gives us information on the days preceeding the siege of the Cité. Threatened by the revolt which was speading through the country, the Archbishop of Narbonne, a number of barons faithful to the King, and some "clercks together with their men and their goods" had taken refuge in the citadel "confident in the feeling of security provided by the town and the faubourg". At the same time, stores were piled up in the town, and "the walls were fortified by wooden structures" (probably hoardings and machines were set up). William of Ormes chose to avoid battle on the open plain, probably because he did not have enough men. To re-establish the balance, he followed the old saying which maintains that a defender is worth three attackers, and he waited for the enemy behind the walls of the Cité. This decision was all the wiser, since the Seneschal knew that he would only need to hold out a certain length of time. The King would not allow his authority to be flouted nor would he permit a minor feudal lord to take part of the royal domain by force, however justified such an act might be. As soon as the revolt began to look serious, William of Ormes sent a messenger to Louis IX at Bourges, informing him of the situation and requesting reinforcements. Just a few hours before Trencavel began to invest the place, the messenger who had been hastily sent to the King was back again, with the information that an army led by Jean of Beaumont had already set out. "The prelates and barons" showed the King's message to the populace "with great joy".

Apparently, William of Ormes did not trust the people of the bourg. On the 7th September, the Seneschal went down to the bourg with the Bishop, and assembled the burgesses and the people in Sainte-Marie Church. He asked them all to swear "on the body of Christ, the saints' relics and the very holy evangelists" to remain faithful to the King and contribute to the defence. But, according to William of Puy-laurens, certain people had already made contact with the enemy, who were only a few miles away. In the night of the 8th to 9th September, Trencavel and his band were let into the bourg, and the population found themselves on the side of the rebels, either because they wanted to or because they were forced to. There was nothing exceptional about managing to get into a town through the treachery of one or more of the inhabitants. Finding allies within the besieged place was one of the options open to the aggressor, and it was often resorted to, since it was a way of economising time, trouble and money. In a society where loyalty was held in the highest esteem, nobody was averse to making use of the traitor. The continuator of the Song finds it quite normal to have Montfort say, when he was trying to free his men from the dungeon of Beaucaire, "if he (the young Count Raymond) refuses to let our barons leave the castle, we will handsomely grease the palms of any of his men who help ours to escape".

On the morning of the 9th September, the enemy was right in front of the Cité walls, but the fighting did not really commence until the 17th, according to William of Ormes. Was Trencavel waiting for other rebel lords to arrive? Did he use this week to assemble and construct the siege equipment he needed and to dig himself in? The report of the seneschal says nothing of this.

William of Ormes' report has been quoted many times, sometimes in full, sometimes using long extracts. Viollet-le-Duc who never missed an opportunity for flattering Napoléon III, used the translation made by Louis-Napoléon Bonaparte for the *Études sur le Passé et l'Avenir de l'Artillerie*, in his *Essai sur l'architecture militaire au Moyen Âge*, and in his dictionary. I hope I shall be forgiven for daring to doubt the competence of the Emperor (or the ghost writer used by him) in his role of Latin scholar. But a careful study of the text reveals that the translator confused *fugare*, to put to flight, with *fugere*, to run away. The Razès Gate becomes the Rodez Gate, thus placing it in the opposite direction, several passages have been skipped, Saturday becomes Sunday, and Thursday becomes Monday... These are perhaps details, but I thought it might be worth attempting a less prestigious but more accurate translation.

Porte du Razès, Plan 16
Porte de Rodez, Plan 4

"Greatings to the excellent and most honourable Lady Blanche, Queen of the French, by the grace of God, from her humble, devoted and faithful servant, William of Ormes, Seneschal of Carcassonne. Let it be brought to your knowledge by those here present that the Cité of Carcassonne was besieged by he who claims to be Viscount and by his supporters, on the Monday following the week of the nativity of Saint Mary. We at the Cité immediately took from them the bourg of Granoillant which is in front of the Toulouse Gate, and we took a great quantity of wood which was of great use to us. That bourg stretches from the barbican of the Cité to the spur. The same day, helped by a great crowd of supporters, the enemy took a mill from us. Then Olivier de Termes, Bernard Hugo de Serre-Longue, Guillaume d'Aniort and their men took up position between the spur of the Cité and the river. The same day, using the ditches in that place and destroying the routes which were between our two sides, they entrenched themselves so well that we could not reach them. Another detachment consisting of Pierre de Fenouillet,

Porte de Toulouse, Plan 11

The West Front of the Cité

In the centre, the covered way which led to the castle barbican, and where William of Ormes positioned his « turkish stone-throwing machine ». On the right, the corne of the Cité, where the enemy managed to mine part of the outside wall.

Barbacane du château, Plan 21

Renaud du Puy, Guillaume Fort, Pierre de la Tour and many others from Carcassonne positioned themselves between the bridge and the castle barbican. They managed to do this as soon as they arrived, and there were so many arbalets in these two places that nobody could leave the Cité without being wounded. Then they set up a mangonel opposite our barbican. We immediately put a very good Turkish stone-throwing machine in our barbican, and with this we fired at the mangonel and all round it, to such good effect that when they prepared to use their mangonel against us and they saw us getting ready our stone-throwing machine, they ran away and completely abandonned the mangonel. They had dug ditches and set up palisades. Although we could not reach them because of the ditches, the sharp stakes and the holes, every time we used the stone-throwing machine we caused them to run away.

Porte Narbonnaise, Plan 1

Moreover, Madame, they began to dig a mine against the barbican of the Narbonne Gate, but as soon as we heard the miners working, we mined against them and we put up a big strong wall of dry stones in the barbican, so as to well protect half of the barbican. Then they lit the fire in the gallery they had built, and once the props were burnt out, a part of the barbican came away. They also began to mine another tower of the lists, we mined against them and we pushed them out from the gallery they had made. Then they began to mine between us and a wall and they turned the lists against us over a length of two crenellations, but we immediately put up a good strong palisade between them and us.

''They also mined the spur of the Cité, near the Bishop's residence. They started digging a long way away and by passing under a Saracen wall they managed to reach the wall of the lists. When we realised what they were doing, we put up a good strong palisade between them and us, even higher in the lists and we mined against them. They fired their gallery and destroyed about ten spans of our crenellation. Then in great haste we built a good strong palisade topped by a good brattice with good arrow-holes. After this they did not dare approach us. Madame, they also undertook to mine the barbican of the Razès Gate and there they went very deep, for they wanted to reach our wall. In that place they built an extraordinarily long corridor. But when we became aware of this we built a good strong palisade in the lists from top to bottom. We also mined against them, and when we met up with them we took their gallery.

Porte du Razès, Plan 16

''You should know also, Madame, that from the beginning of the siege they continually made assaults on us. But we had quantities of excellent crossbows as well as brave people determined to defend themselves. As a result, the enemy lost many men each time they attacked. One Sunday, they assembled all their soldiers, the crossbowmen and the others, and all together they attacked the barbican below the castle. We all went down as far as the barbican and we threw so many stones at them and fired so many quarrels that they retreated with many dead and wounded. The following Saturday, after Saint Michael's Day, they made a very big attack. Thanks to God and to the our people who were determined to defend their town we managed to push them back. Many of the enemy were wounded or killed, whereas on our side, thanks be to God there were no dead or seriously wounded. Then, Madame, on the following Thursday evening they learnt that your reinforcements were coming to our aid. They set fire to the houses in the bourg of Carcassonne and entirely destroyed the lodgings of the Frères Mineurs and of the convent of Sainte-Marie, which were in the bourg and whose wood they had taken to make their palisades. All those who had taken part in the siege retreated furtively during the night, including those of the bourg. I must say, Madame, that by the grace of God, we were well prepared to wait for your aid. In spite of the siege, even the poorest were not without food. In fact, Madame, it was quite the opposite, for we had vast quatities of corn and meat which would have enabled us to wait a very long time for your reinforcements, if that had been necessary.

"You should know, Madame, that on the day after they arrived in the bourg, those same malefactors killed thirty-three priests and the clerks whom they had found there.

"You should know, Madame, that the lord Pierre de Voisins, your Constable for Carcassonne, and Raymond de Capendu, and Gérard d'Ermenville, conducted themselves very well in this affaire. But I must say that I would place the Constable above all others for his vigilance, and his courage in fighting and in defence. As for the situation in the region, I shall describe that to you when I am in your presence. As for the situation in the region, I shall describe that to you when I am in your presence.

"In conclusion I should add that they began to mine seriously in seven places and that we mined against them with all our energy whenever it was necessary. They began to dig from their houses so that we could detect nothing until they reached our lists.

"Written in Carcassonne on the 3rd of the Ides of October.

"Be aware, Madame, that the enemy burnt the castles and the villages which they found when they fled."

This long text needs a few explanations. The Cité defences as described here are not the same as those existing in 1209. It is true that the old Gallo-Roman wall was

probably still there, but now we hear of lists, of list towers, of barbicans... which quite clearly did not exist when the Crusaders took the town. Up till now no written document has been discovered mentioning fortification works which took place between 1209 and 1240. But this missive of William of Ormes leaves us in no doubt that the Gallo-Roman wall had been doubled by a second wall. The word *lice* (list) is sometimes used to designate an outer wall ("a tower of the lists", "the length of two crenellations of the lists"...), sometimes for the space between the walls ("higher in the lists", "at the top and the bottom"...). This use of the word with a double meaning is normal practice. We shall come back to this problem in the following chapter, but here we can say that it is most probable that the wall and the towers of the lists mentioned in the text are more or less the outside city wall which we see today. Barbicans have been added to the Narbonne Gate, in the east, and to the Razès Gate in the south. We do not know what the gates looked like on the interior wall because they have since

Porte Narbonnaise, Plan 1
Porte du Razès, Plan 16

Rocks found at Carcassonne

These rocks or bolts, propelled by mangonels and other stone-throwing machines, weighed between 90 and 220 lbs.

been much altered. The outside wall goes out in a semi-circle at this point to create a larger area and provide an advanced defence position. The "castle barbican" also refers to a fortification in an advanced position, but it is of a different type. It is the big circular fortification placed at the end of the covered route (that is to say closed in by two walls), which today leads down from the castle gate to Church of Saint-Gimer.

Barbacane du château, Plan 21

Chemin couvert, Plan 20

William of Ormes refers to the bourg of Granoillant, "in front of the Toulouse Gate", today known as the Aude Gate. This bourg, which was in the south-east part of the outskirts of the Cité, seems to have grown since 1209 when it was probably little more than a hamlet. William of Ormes was not referring to the bourg of Saint-Michel, situated to the south-east. This bourg had been taken by the Crusaders in 1209 and, according to the Song, completely destroyed. But in the Middle Ages, settlements emerged very quickly from their ruins, and the destruction mentioned by the chroniclers were often less serious they would have us believe. It is certainly the inhabitants of the two bourgs of Saint-Michel and Saint-Vincent, chased from their homes in 1240, who, in 1247, made up the two main parishes of the Lower Town. It is therefore difficult to conclude categorically that the bourg of Saint-Michel no longer existed. The bourg of Saint-Vincent, in the north-east, is the one where the Seneschal assembled the population and made them swear loyalty, and where the rebels entered the following day. The reference by William of Puylaurens to the Sainte-Marie Church, and by the Seneschal to the Sainte-Marie convent, leave us in no doubt about this identification, since this church is none other then the church of Our Lady, situated today on the north flank of the mound in the part of the town known as Trivalle. If "the point of the Cité", cor-

Porte de Toulouse, Plan 11

nu, in latin, refers without any doubt to the south angle where the bishop's palace was effectively located, other expressions in the Seneschal's report remains extremely obscure and the exact location of the mining works, vague or inexistent. Which of the list towers was mined? What is meant by the phrase "they mined between us and the wall"? What is the "Saracen wall" (Gallo-Roman constructions are often referred to in this way), under which the mining gallery passed? Moreover, after describing 5 attempts, William of Ormes adds that the fortifications were mined in 7 different places!

The sequence of operations, however, presents no problems. It would seem that Trencavel began by trying to ensure that the defenders had no access to the river. To do this he seized a mill surrounded "by an old, straggly fence" (William of Puylaurens), and massacred the young people he found there. He held on carefully to the approaches to the Aude on both sides of the castle barbican. Fearing sorties on the part of the defenders, the besiegers took shelter behind the trenches and the fences. As we have seen from our study of the three other sieges, defence in the 13th century was not simply a matter of waiting patiently behind the walls. When the inhabitants of the bourg joined the rebellion, Trencavel had a large pool of potential man-power at his disposal. It is true that they were not equipped or trained for combat, but they could at least wield a spade and pickaxe. This transfer of allegiance also meant that the walls were not mined in the way they had been in 1209, but by the underground method, "in the fashion of moles" says William of Puylaurens. This was made possible because the possession of the bourg houses enabled the miners to work without being seen.

We have seen how mining operations carried out on the surface with the limit-

L'Aude, Plan 23

The east entrance to the Count's Castle
A solid protection turned against an unreliable population.

ed protection of a *chatte* were more risky than underground mining, but the latter could also be detected by the enemy because of the vibrations in the ground caused by the blows. The defenders therefore went underground to meet the enemy and to fight them, or as William of Puylaurens says, to dislodge them "by smoke and quicklime". The troops of William of Ormes appear to have been well skilled in this technique. They were also very good at rapidly constructing a palisade of dry stones at the back of the wall which was in danger. The attacks launched by Trencavel were not crowned with success, nor did they come anywhere near succeeding. William of Ormes, moreover, emphasises the fact that he suffered few losses. One of the first historians of the Crusade[9] wrote: "After a month of siege, Carcassonne was almost completely reduced to desperation", this was, to say the least, a pessimistic point of view.

In the Cité, the fighting was carried out by the Seneschal, his Constable, Peter of Voisins, a small group of crossbow sergeants (although the town did not yet have a permanent garrison of any importance) and a few of the King's men-at-arms, who hade been chased from their castles and from their positions by the rebellion. The main part of the defence should have been carried out by the *terrari*, knights who, accompanied by their squires and valets, had to guard a part of the city defences and go to their suzerain's aid, in return for the land they had received in fief. Few carried out their duty, some even went over to the opposite camp. Although there were not very many of them, the defenders were competent, determined men; what they managed to accomplish proves this. William of Ormes emphasises this "determination to defend". When the arrival of the army commanded by Jean of Beaumont was announced on Thursday 11th October

in the evening, the besiegers immediately fled, "setting fire to various parts of the bourg and abandonning it to the French".

But the failure of this revolt was to have far more important consequences for Carcassonne. First of all for the man who considered himself Viscount of this town. He took refuge in Catalunia, and later, in 1242, took part in another insurrection led by Raymond VII of Toulouse against the Crown. This rebellion also ended in failure. Finally, on 22nd August 1246, Raymond Trencavel asked for the King's pardon and for his excommunication to be lifted. The King demanded that the Viscount surrender all his property titles. He then granted Trencavel a considerable pension and invited him with great urgency to participate in the Crusade he was going to conduct in Egypt. Trencavel accepted these conditions on 7th April 1247, and to show that he renounced his former possessions, he broke his seal. It seem that he did actually go to fight the Infidels and that as a reward for his bravery, he got back some of his lands in Terménès. A document of December 1269 tells us that one of his sons, Roger of Béziers, agreed to accompany the King on his second expedition to the Holy Land with six knights and four crossbowmen. Roger received 200 livres minted at Tours as an advance payment for his participation in the Crusade. After that we lose trace of the Trencavels.

The second consequence of the revolt of 1240 and of its failure, was the very harsh repression which fell on the country. From October to December 1240, Jean of Beaumont pursued the remaining rebels. He punished the towns and villages which had declared their support for Trencavel, and seized the pockets of resistance. "The extinction and dispossession of the old, seigneurial families dates from this pitiless campaign", writes Charles Victor Langlois in *Histoire de*

France by Ernest Lavisse. The bourgs around the Cité, or what was left of them, were entirely razed, leaving only the last remains of a few gates to survive for a short time. As for the inhabitants, all they could do was to hide in the surrounding countryside and villages and wait for the King's pardon wich was long in coming.

The fate of the Trencavel was to coincide one more time with that of Carcassonne. When Raymond Trencavel solemnly gave up his possessions in 1247 and received his pardon, Saint Louis extended his forgiveness to the inhabitants of the bourgs, with the exception of the leaders. At the beginning of 1248, the inhabitants were invited to return to the bourg on condition that they did not build anything on the hill overlooking the Cité. The royal seneschals had learnt their lesson from the siege of 1240, and they had no intention of letting mine galleries be constructed from the houses near the walls, nor of allowing alleyways be used to give cover to the enemy right until the last minute, nor of enabling the attackers to use resting places, supplies and wood, right under their noses. Now that it was free of its bourgs, the Cité could fulfil its military vocation. The important modifications and the grand constructions of the 13th century reflect this role.

The end of a dynasty

Trencavel gave up his lands. In 1269, one of his sons,
Roger of Béziers, received 200 livres tournois as an advance payment of what
he would receive for accompanying Louis IX overseas with six knights
and four crossbowmen.

THE DEFENCES

Keeping hold of Languedoc and opposing the Kingdom of Aragon

The former possession of the Trencavels became the most important part of the royal lands in Languedoc after two major events: the transfer by Amaury de Montfort of his rights over the South to the King, and the Crusade of 1226, led by Louis VIII. After this, the defence of the Cité, which had become the seat of a seneschalchy, fell to the Crown. The majority of the walls and towers visible today were constructed by royal order and bear the mark of that origin. These buildings reflect the policy begun by Philip II, which was to occupy recently acquired lands, consolidate the power of the Crown by building, and cut short any attempt to question the annexations which had taken place.

In the context of Languedoc, these precautions were justified. The first priority was to keep hold of an important region, since it gave the king access to the Mediterranean for the first time. However, the Languedoc country was known to be unreliable, as had been fully illustrated by the revolt of 1240. The "resistance" continued until the fall of the last Cathar centres, that of Montségur in 1244, and Quéribus in 1255. As late as 1275, the Viscount of Narbonne was plotting against the "French occupiers". On the other hand, if the battle of Muret had put a break on Aragonese expansion, it had not completely crushed it. The kings of Aragon acted prudently, but always paid great attention to what was happening in the South. They offered sanctuary to Raymond Trencavel and did nothing to dissuade him from trying to regain his lands. If it had not been for the swift reaction of Louis IX in crushing the coalition between the English and Toulouse in 1242 (a movement in which Trencavel participated), James II of Aragon might also have joined the uprising.

The Treaty of Corbeil (May 1258), a compromise for both parties, seems to have put as end to this period of tension between France and Aragon. On his side, Louis IX admitted that he had no rights over Catalunia, Cerdagne and Roussillon (formerly the borderland with Spain, set up by Charlemagne); he was thus no longer the suzerain, however theoretical, of the King of Aragon. In return, the latter renounced his rights over Carcassès, Razès, Biterrois, Lauragais... In this way he implicitly gave up his ambition of creating a state across the Pyrenees. From then on, the frontier between the two kingdoms was clear. It passed through the Corbières and the Pas de Salses, more or less following the route which today goes from Quillan to Perpignan, bordering the contemporary departments of the Aude and the Pyrénées Orientales. As the first big town at the entry to the upper valley of the Aude, Carcassonne became the heart of the defence system for the Franco-Aragonese frontier, situated only fifty kilometres away.

Twenty-five years later, Carcassonne, which was already a key defence city, also became a hinterland base for an extremely important expedition, the Aragon Crusade. This was the first expedition that the Capetians were to lead outside the kingdom. By diverting the King of Aragon from his ambitions in the North, the Treaty of Corbeil revived this dynasty's interest in Mediterranean affairs. In 1282, the "Sicilian Vespers" put an end to a brief spell of Angevin domination in Sicily. The court of Aragon had played a part in this popular revolt and Peter III became "King of Sicily and Palermo". From that moment, in France, Charles of Anjou intrigued to have his revenge on the man who had dispossessed him. In this he received the unqualified support of the Pope, Martin IV. The French court debat-

The inside of the Castle

A section of the main part of the central lodge with the kitchens in the basement. To the left, on the inner side of the wall, an outhouse, which may have been used for sheltering the horses. Above, the hoardings. To the right, the Midi courtyard, half of which is still taken up by the remains of a building. Drawing by Viollet-le-Duc.

ed whether to go to war against Aragon. In the spring of 1285, the King took the lead of a very powerful army. He made a halt at Carcassonne, where he left the Queen, Mary of Brabant, and the other ladies of the court. The Cité seemed the last secure place before the adventure to come. The campaign did not last long. The army managed to cross the Pyrenees, but decimated by malaria and deprived of supplies following the destruction of the accompanying fleet, and had to retreat. Philip III himself fell ill and died at Perpignan in October 1285.

The work of the royal architects

It is not in the least surprising that Carcassonne became an exceptionally powerful royal fortress in the course of the 13th century. The fortifications were the answer to the most common form of medieval wars, "a succession of sieges, together with a multitude of skirmishes and devastations and the occasional major battle". In this siege warfare, the urban centres, more than the castles, played a crucial role. By virtue of their administrative, economic and cultural functions, and

The siege the Cité never experienced
After 1240, there were no more serious attacks on the Cité.
However, arms were stocked in the castle.
This 15th century miniature shows tower
crossbows and mortars.

of the number and quality of the populations they sheltered, they were the "true masters of the region" (Philip Contamine)[10]. From the reign of Philip Augustus, a group of royal engineers went to work throughout the country, in Montreuil, Compiègne, Laon, Rouen, Caen, Bourges, Loudun to ensure that the royal domain was well defended. They were called *magister, cementarius* or *fossator* (specialist in terracing works), and went from one site to another, alone or in a group, and they almost always followed the same principles and used the same ideas for their architecture.

At Carcassonne there is a dearth of written sources which might help us pieced together the history of the major alteration and construction works carried out in the 13th century. In 1436 the town hall of the bourg (that is of the Lower Town) was burnt down, along with all the archives it contained. In September 1793, all the archives stored in the Count's castle went up in flames during a fire celebrating the Revolution. For this period, archeologists must depend on their own careful observation, crosschecking, comparisons with other monuments, and on a few rare texts.

The building material used was, without any doubt, of local origin. It is sandstone, usually greyish in colour, but sometimes yellow or ochre when mixed with iron oxides. The grain is sometimes fine and will crumble into very light dust as a result of wind erosion. But it is sometimes so coarse that one can distinguish the tiny pieces of grit. It might have been extracted from the mound itself or from neighbouring quarries, which have not been precisely located, but which could not have been more than a few kilometres from the Cité. We know nothing about the men who cut, transported and assembled the stone.

The architects came from the King's en-

tourage, but the workforce was most probably recruited locally. A large number of workmen must have been employed, because, in contrast to the cathedrals, which, for lack of money, took over a century to build, the fortifications were completed in a surprisingly short time. In 1155, Pisa was surrounded by a trench six kilometres long; the major part of the Château-Gaillard was constructed in one year (1197); the enormous Harlech Castle in Wales was completed in seven years (1283-1290). In 1286 the following number of workmen were on the Welsh site: 227 masons, 115 stone-cutters, 30 blacksmiths, 22 carpenters, 4 clerks, 546 unskilled workers and pieceworkers. The cost of operations at Harlech in one year alone amounted to 1600 *livres*, equivalent to a fifth of the wool tax for the whole of England[11].

The Later Empire wall

Unfortunately we do not have such royal accounts for Carcassonne, and so it is very

Puylaurens
One of the « five sons of Carcassonne » guarding the French-Aragonese frontier. Carcassonne became the centre of an important network of military defences against Aragon.

difficult to put a more precise date on the different construction campaigns.

The basic structure of the stronghold was built little by little, throughout the 13th century. At the time of the Crusade, the Cité was only protected by the Later Empire wall. The ground plan of that wall corresponds almost exactly with that of the present inside wall, except near the **Tour du Trésau, Plan 2** Trésau Tower, where excavations have shown that it was further back and near the Mipadre Tower, in the south angle in front of the tower. The oval shape followed the relief of the rocky spur on which the town is built. It is different from **Porte nord, Plan 4** the rectangular ground plan usual in Gallo-Roman walls, although the same shape is found at Senlis. But the positioning of the exits at the four cardinal points is standard. The North Gate and the Aude **Porte d'Aude, Plan 11** Gate (in the west) undoubtedly correspond to the approaches existing in the Later Empire. In the south, the alterations carried out on the wall during the reign of Philip III prevent us from making any precise guess at location; **Tour Saint-Nazaire, Plan 16** we can only suppose that the Saint-Nazaire Gate is located along the original south passage.

For the same reason, it is difficult to accurately locate the gate facing the east; it was probably not very far from the Narbonne Gate. Since it opened onto the only **Porte Narbonnaise, Plan 1** side of the hill used by carts, we can assume that it was better defended than the other gates. Two posterns are still visible. **Tour Pinte, Plan 8** The one at the base of the Pinte Tower is walled up, whereas the passage of the second, know as the Avar Postern was cleared some years ago. By walking along this passage one can appreciate the thickness of the walls: a good nine feet thick.

The outside of the postern is made of huge blocks, used for the foundations as well. The wall is built on a bed of mortar surmounted by one or two layers of big blocks. These foundations, which are not very deep (about five feet), are visible today in several places. They were discovered during repair works in the 13th century. The interior of the wall, made of a thick block of compressed sand, stones and lime, is extremely resistant. The surface of the walls is faced with small stonework, less regularly arranged than in other Gallo-Roman fortifications of the Later Empire. The stonework is crossed with chains of brickwork or, in the case of the Saint-Sernin Tower, with bricks arranged in fish-bone shape *(opus spicatum,* like a herring bone). This arrangement, which was common in buildings of the Later Empire, was undoubtedly used to provide a perfectly flat surface for the next layer of bricks. At Carcassonne these chains are used very irregularly. One explanation of this is that, due to the urgency, the builders were not perfectionists. Another is that this was a later, not very successful imitation (by the Visigoths) of Roman techniques. The walls, which are between 18 and 25 feet high, are topped by a crenellation with merlons but without loopholes (arrow-slits). Every 20 or 30 yards (the distance depending on the degree of "natural" defence at each point), there are horse-shoe shaped towers, flat on the side facing the town, semi-circular on the exterior. These towers are filled in up to the level of the first floor, thus constituting an enormous block of masonry, acting as a support for the wall, but also capable of bringing the wall down with it. On the first level, three windows

Building
These two 14th century paintings clearly show the building techniques used at the time. We see the crane, the straw used for ciment, the putlog holes used for putting up the scaffolding. Galerie Franchetti, Venice.

open out onto the surrounding countryside. The semi-circular arches of the windows are decorated, like the doors, with brick archstones. The level above, made of wood, acts as a passageway for the posts in the crenellation. It is not sure that these towers were covered, at least not in the earliest times. The absence of a vault made it possible to do without a roof, which would act as a protection against the rain. Vegetius simply recommended that *"guérites" (tuguriola,* small cabins) should be built on the walls and towers for the comfort of the soldiers. Slings and the *pilum,* a javelin six feet long, consisting of a wooden staff attached to an iron spear, could be thrown from the windows and the battlements.

When the enemy was not too powerful, the massive, solid walls of the Later Empire, with their shooting facilities, provided excellent protection. They were completed by some wooden additions like the covered galleries *(ambans)* on the guard route, from which Roger Trencavel watched the Crusaders in amazement. Would they have been able to keep the Crusaders out for long in 1209? William of Tudèle thought so. But twenty years later, the royal engineers took no notice of the poet's opinion. They considered that it was essential to alter the defences of the Cité in a significant way. Simon de Montfort, who spent his time travelling round the country and was always short of money, did not have the means to be a great builder. When the Cité was annexed to the royal domain in 1226, a new period of important works began, but, because of the scarcity of surviving documents, it is not always possible to give a precise date to the different stages.

The Castle

The first seneschal, Adam de Milly, and his men took up residence in the Count's Castle, and it is probably here that the first alterations were made. At the beginning of the 12th century, the *palatium* of the Trencavels had replaced the Narbonne Castle, a building situated near the east gate of the town, probably behind the Saint-Sernin Tower, and of which nothing now remains, except the references to it in a few charters. The new residence was situated opposite the fortifed perimeter, on the extreme west of the mound, in the place best protected by the natural lie of the land. It consisted of two main buildings. The first backed onto the Gallo-Roman wall and ended in two big, square towers, sometimes called dungeons. The second came out at a rectangle to the city wall. The whole formed an L-shape, and enclosed a courtyard, which was more or less shut off from the town. The building was one storey high and had a *"lauzes"* (stone) roof, bordered with a crenellated parapet. The Pinte Tower was built by Bernard Aton a few metres to the south. The tower was a symbol of the seigneur's power, and was put there to be seen from afar, as much as to observe the countryside it dominated. Our Lady's Chapel, *"juxta palatium",* was put up to the north, in about the year 1160. One of the Gallo-Roman towers of the wall served as apse to the chapel.

"Donjons", Plan 7

Tour Pinte, Plan 8

Pierre Héliot was the first to demonstrate that the castle *"chemise",* that is the fortified walls which surround it on three sides, could not have been built earlier than the beginning of the 13th century[12]. The regular layout, the towers which project sharply from the walls, the possibility of "hoarding" the walls and towers, the positioning and the shape of the arrow-slits, and the very elaborate east gate, are all characteristic of the progress made by military architecture in the North and West of France in the reign of Philip Augustus. Pierre Héliot logically suggests that the date should be set be-

tween 1226 and 1245. This period can probably be limited to the first years after Carcassonne was annexed to the royal domain, if we follow the conclusions of Yves Bruand[13]. The castle walls should be seen as a fortification turned against the town. The seneschal and his men, who occupied the former residence of the Trencavels and Montforts, were confronted with a hostile population, and probably felt in need of fortifications which would offer them protection in time of riots or plots. The revolt of 1240 and the attitude of at least part of the bourg population, who welcomed and aided Raymond Trencavel, were later to justify these fears.

The Castle Hoardings

These overhanging galleries enabled the defenders to throw missiles down to the base of the wall, and were particularly useful against sappers. The base of the wall is en fruit *(on a slight incline), so that the fall from the hoarding holes is perfectly straight.*

An innovative defence system

It may have been just after this first fortification campaign that a semi-circular barbican was erected, constituting a first obstacle to the enemy and providing an open space within shooting range of the castle archers behind this first line of defence. (The barbican was subsequently rebuilt rather than restored except for the central part which is original.) A wide ditch, now crossed by a stone bridge, and before by moveable wooden planks and a drawbridge system, cut off the approach to the siege engines and larger *chattes*. When the war engines were pushed to the edge of the counterscarp, they crashed into the ditch. However, it was possible for sappers to take the risk of jumping down into the ditch and approaching the walls, under the protection of their shields. To limit this danger, great care was taken in flanking the wall. The towers which are round on the exterior had no blind angles; they came out quite a way from the wall and the archers were able to shoot parallel to the wall. The arrow slits, which began on the lower storey, were arranged in quincunz from one level to the next, so as to increase the number of directions for shooting, and so as not to weaken the construction in any one place. They were splayed outwards and ended in a stirrup, and provided excellent angles for shooting. Along the top of the towers and curtain wall, the hoards provided a continuous vertical flanking. These wooden galleries were probably not always in position, but could be rapidly erected, using the rectangular holes built into the crenellated parapet. Beams could be placed in the holes, and thus made an outside overhanging passageway.

By climbing over the embrasures, it was possible to go from the sentry-route onto the wooden floor of the hoardings. These were open all along, enabling the

defenders to throw all kinds of missiles down onto the enemy at the base of the wall: stones, planks, logs... Since the base of the walls and the towers sloped slightly, the enemy was immediately below the openings in the hoardings. This helped protect the building against sapping. The gate defence system seems to have been extremely innovative. According to Pierre Héliot, these different elements were gradually introduced in the North and the West of France, from the beginning of the 13th century onwards. Around the year 1230, at the same time that the royal engineers were beginning the important construction works at Carcassonne, Angers and Boulogne-sur-mer (the gate of degrees) were built. The two twin towers, linked by a central lodge, over the en-

trance, constituted a little castle in itself. The attacker had to get through a first system consisting of a machicoulis hidden by a semi-circular arch, then a portcullis and then a heavy door. After this he then came up against a second system, similar to the first, and consisting of machicoulis, portcullis and door. These machicoulis were used to reach those attackers who persisted in trying to force the portcullis, and also to seize the girders of battering-rams in a noose and to immobilise them by dragging them upwards, as suggested by Vegetius. Finally they were used to pour down the water needed to put out any attempt at setting fire to the door. A last precaution reveals the fear of treason. The leverage system of the first portcullis is situated on the

The Castle

*With its rectangular lay-out and its very elaborate defence system,
the castle appears as the royal citadel dominating the town.*

second floor of the central lodge, where one can still distinguish in the ground the opening of the machicoulis and the slit for letting the portcullis slide down, whereas the second portcullis and second machicoulis were controlled from the first storey and so entrusted to a team of different guards.

The success of an escalade, that is, the fact that a few men had managed to get a foothold on the curtain wall did not mean that the system of defences broke down. The defence system was in fact split up in a remarkable way. The towers interrupted the sentry-route, the level of the walls suddenly changed. This made it difficult to reach and to get over the walls and meant that the enemy was prevented from gaining control of the next part of the wall. At the south and north corners, the passage is so narrow, that it could easily be blocked up. Finally, the guards on the upper levels always had the sentry-route within range of their arrows. The different levels communicated with each other via staircases running the length of the interior side of the wall, or by trap-doors through the vault or in the floor of the last storey, or in the case of the corner towers, by means of a spiral staircase. The depressed domed vaults seem a little archaic, but the fixtures were very carefully designed. The alcoves built into the wall gave more room to the archers and enabled the archers and the cross-bowmen to handle their arms with greater ease. This last innovation was hardly seen before 1230.

The Count's Castle had no opening onto the town fortifications and was indeed totally independent from it. It had its own water supply (a dep well on the north-east corner of the Midi courtyard), its own bakery (the bread ovens are still visible in the wall of the building backing onto the Gallo-Roman wall). All these features make the castle look like a citadel with a

defence system which was extremely modern for the beginning of the 13th century. In fact, until the end of the 12th century, the towers and walls of the fortifications were practically blind and defence operations were conducted from the heights; walls were rarely flanked by regularly spaced, projecting towers. Here we see that the number of arrow-slits had been increased, not only on the curtain wall at the level of the courtyard, but on nearly all the levels of the towers. They are the first signs of a change in the conception of defence. Instead of remaining essentially passive, instead of relying almost exclusively on the walls to repel the attacker, defence now became more active and more concerned to inflict a maximum of losses on the enemy.

An inner wall tower
These are sometimes «open at the throat» (not blocked in on the interior), so that the enemy would be exposed, if they managed to take the tower.

The second fortification campaign

This new philosophy of defence, together with the traditional objective of making the enemy's task more difficult, also guided the royal engineers in the second phase of fortification works. This phase mainly concerned the town, and either took place at the same time, or a little after the construction of the castle *chemise*. It be remembered that the report of the Seneschal William of Ormes mentions the existence of lists, list towers and crenellation, barbicans, and castle barbicans. There is every reason to suppose that the elements described are more or less those we see today and that the outer wall, as we know it, was built before 1240.

The doubling of city walls was never very common. In the case of Carcassonne, it can be explained by the unstable political situation existing in the first years of the French occupation. The destruction of the existing walls with a view to replacing them by more modern fortifications, would have been a way of offering ready-made breaches to the enemy, even if the work had been carried out in stages. Moreover, the natural lie of the land would not have encouraged the builder to stray far from the existing ground plan. If the city wall had been extended to go round the base of the hill and thus surround the whole settlement including the two bourgs, as was often done when a new wall was built, the advantage of a dominant position would have been lost, and the few reliable defenders would have been scattered over too wide an area and mixed up with the restless inhabitants of the bourgs. The quality of the fortifications dating from the Later Empire must also have been an important factor in the debate. The walls were certainly ''out of date'', but there was nothing flimsy about them; on the contrary, they formed a strong, solid defence system.

Since the existing wall had obvious advantages, but could not be counted on to offer total protection, it became tempting to think in terms of constructing a second outer wall in place of the palisades, sentry-boxes and the wooden turret which were normally put up in front of the walls in times of danger. This would force the enemy to double its attacks and mining operations. It would also make mining more difficult because the attackers would have to dig under a first wall in order to reach the second (in 1240 the rebels did not manage to do this without being detected), and then succeed in bringing down both walls at the same time. Another advantage was that a second line of archers and crossbowmen could be stationed on the outer wall which was always designed to be lower than the inner wall. This system of defence was more complex but more efficient. On the side of the rocky spur which was not so well protected by the natural lie of the land, a ditch, about twelve feet deep, was dug alongside the outer wall. Like the castle moat, it was a dry ditch, since it was impossible to bring the water up the sides of the hill and keep it there. On the west side, from the gates of the bourg in the north to Saint-Nazaire in the south, the rock was sheer enough to prevent any siege engines from approaching.

The outer rampart is about one and an half kilometre long. The walls are made of medium-sizes stones put together fairly roughly, and reach a height of 20 to 30 feet. They are flanked with about 15 towers, as well as a few watch towers on the corners, and the barbicans of the gates. At the main entrances, the wall bulges out in a semi-circle, offering enough space for stationing the soldiers and equipment needed to defend these strategic points. The report of the siege of 1240 shows that these projections provided a margin of security for the defenders, for when a

Porte du bourg, Plan 4
Tour Saint-Nazaire, Plan 16

mining operation caused a part of the Narbonne Gate barbican to collapse, the defenders quickly built a wall further back and were thus able to keep half of their **Porte Narbonnaise, Plan 1** position. To reach the Narbonne Gate, it was probably necessary to cross a fixed or moveable bridge. The drawbrige in front of the town was very rare before the 14th century, so it is difficult to understand the reasoning behind the "restoration" conjured up by Boeswillwald. The North Gate leads into the ditch and the South Gate opens onto the end of the **Porte d'Aude, Plan 11** ditch. The Aude or Toulouse Gate in the west is not protected by a barbican, which would have been impossible to construct because of the lie of the land. Here, protection is provided by a wall parallel **Avant-porte d'Aude, Plan 12** to the outer wall, so that along several feet, the route known as the *"montée d'Aude"* is safeguarded by two walls.

The mostly semi-circular towers are spaced out at intervals of between 30 and 50 yards, sometimes more. This was perfectly adequate since the crossbows had a range of about a hundred yards. Some towers, particularly those on the southeast face are open on the side facing the town. In this way, attackers, who had managed to take the towers, were exposed to the arrows coming from the second line of defence, and could not use the towers as a refuge. They were only one storey high. On the north side, the towers are more elaborate with a vaulted storey and low rooms well below the level of the lists.

The lists and modifications to the inner wall

This is the way the space between the two walls is used. According to Georges Duby[14], in the tournaments held at that time the lists were called "barriers where men went to rest. The lists marked off the places of refuge, the recess... where the combattants had the right to take

Wood and Iron

Putting up the hoardings. The portcullis leverage mechanism. Drawings by Viollet-le-Duc.

**Porte rouge,
Plan 5**

shelter for a bit and catch their breath…''.

Yves Bruand considers that important works were carried out to level the lists at the same time as the outer wall was constructed. If the natural slope of the ground on the mound had not been modified, the area between the two walls would have been very steep and it would not have been easy to move around. It is highly probable though not certain that the earthworks aimed at levelling out the lists were executed at this period. In his report, William of Ormes writes of palisades which were constructed ''higher up'' (*superius*, in the upper part) in the lists or ''up and down'' (*superius* and *in-ferius*). This leads us to assume that the area was on a slope. Moreover, the outer wall on the north-west side, near the Red Gate, has been rebuilt; when looking at the wall from the side of the hill, one can clearly distinguish the traces of the former crenellation and the hoardings holes. It would seem that the earth taken from the foot of the inside defences and placed against the inside wall in order to level out the slope, was piled up to the level of the first line of crenellation, making it necessary to elevate the latter. Yet, if the two operations were carried out at the same time, then the outside defence would surely have been built up to a sufficient

Underpinning works

*To make the lists as level as possible, the depth of the soil at the base of the inner
wall was reduced, with the result that the wall and towers had to be
progressively propped up and extended under the foundations.
Drawing by J.-C. Golvin.*

were altered, and the aim of the works carried out was to make the lists relatively flat. When the earth was taken from the bottom of the Gallo-Roman walls and towers, their foundations were exposed. The whole of the defences therefore had to be underpinned and extended underneath.

The medieval architects were masters of this technique, but nevertheless made a few mistakes. Part of the wall near the North Gate has collapsed, the Marquière Tower leans over to one side, the Vieulas tips forward, even if it has not completely toppled over. The royal engineers rebuilt the upper storey on the base which was on an incline. The upper parts of the fortification were also modified: most of the wall was heightened, the battlements were rebuilt and certain windows in the towers were changed into arrow-slits.

Porte nord, Plan 4

The defences on the west front

As well as the construction of the outer wall, the probable alteration of the Later Empire wall and the erection of the castle *chemise*, the period of 1230 witnessed improvements in the defences on the west face of the castle, where the defences coincide with the inner wall. The Powder Tower, flanking the west gate of the castle, replaces a Gallo-Roman tower (perhaps the one known as the *Tour de la Monnaie*), which has completely disappeared leaving no trace. For practical reasons, towers were not built on the north-west and south-west corners of the castle. At the north-west corner, the curtain wall had to go round the Sainte-Marie Chapel, and so could not abut against the tower which acted as the apse of this little church, but joined up with the inner wall as near as possible. In the south-west, the proximity of the Pinte Tower prevented the construction of a corner tower. This part of the castle is pro-

Tour de la Poudre, Plan 6

Tour Pinte, Plan 8

height. In the north lists, the levelling is far from perfect. It is limited by the outside defences which are too low, and because it was impossible to go too far down when uncovering the original fortification. Finally we have the comment of G. Besse in his *Histoire des antiquitez et comtes de Carcassonne* (Béziers, 1645). He writes that, after the siege of 1240, the royal engineers altered ''the great wall which had not been ruined''. Besse, however, should be treated with caution.

Whether before or after 1240, what it sure is that the Later Empire defences

The Vieulas Tower
The underpinning works on the North front were sometimes carried too far. This tower was put out of balance and began to lean forward. The major part still leans forward, but the upper storey has been rebuilt.

tected by the Justice Tower, built on the site of a Gallo-Roman tower of the inner wall. With their ribbed vaults (particularly elegant in the case of the first floor of

the Justice Tower), the Powder Tower and the Justice Tower are representative of the beautiful, well finished constructions of the middle of the century, during the personal reign of Saint Louis.

The last defence element on the west face, the castle barbican, played, an im-

portant role in the siege of 1240. It was there that the Seneschal's men set up the "Turkish missile-throwing machine'', and it was there that they decided not to make a sortie, because they knew that the enemy was entrenched behind the palisades and ditches. This barbican, which was demolished in 1816 to supply stones for the rebuilding of the spinning-mill of the island, was a big, circular construction, which ensured that control of the Aude

banks was never entirely lost. It was

connected to the lists by a covered way (closed in by two high walls), which still exists. This covered route enabled the defenders to make sorties down to the river. Such sorties down the slope which is very steep in this spot, would have been much more difficult with no protection. Along the last few yards of this route, just before reaching the castle, Viollet-le-Duc decided to put up boarded storeys, rather unconvincing. The west gate of the castle was very probably surmounted by a wooden piece furnished with bludgeons. The wooden piece was supported by a semicircular stone arch, which rested on the Powder Tower to one side, and on a crosspiece pierced with machicoulis to the other.

After the siege of 1240...

With its well protected castle (*castrum* writes William of Ormes and no longer *palatium*, which is the term most

commonly used in documents written during the Trencavel period), and its double walls, the Cité was very different in appearance from what it had been in 1209. The failure of the siege of 1240 was proof of the effectiveness of the new defence system, but also revealed certain weaknesses. It was, of course, necessary to repair the destruction caused by Raymond Trencavel's miners. The Narbonne Gate Barbican (today the Saint-

Louis Barbican) was rebuilt. The reconstruction of that part of the curtain wall which had collapsed on the south-west corner probably resulted in the erection of the Grand Burlas Tower which seems

stronger than the other towers in that part. The north and north-east façade were also repaired. According to Yves Bruand the Benazet Tower on the north-east side was remodelled. If the levelling of the lists and the subsequent modifications of the walls were not carried out in the first stage of building around 1230, it is to this second period that we should attribute them. The problems caused by the slope of the land must have become obvious during the siege, when reinforcements, arms and munitions had to be brought up to counter the attacks launched against the outer wall. Finally, it became clear that the proximity of the bourgs constituted a serious danger, particularly since the enemy could use the houses in the bourgs as departure points for their mining operations.

As we know, the bourgs were immediately destroyed, and the stones from the flattened bourgs were used in the repair works of the outer wall. The mound in the south-west, on which the bourg of Saint-Michel was built, constituted a danger. It rose up almost to the height of the walls. It was at this time that the outer wall curtain was rebuilt and the Vade Tower and the Peyre Tower constructed. The Peyre Tower protected the outlet of an under-

ground communication trench which led beneath the two walls out into the ditch. This tower also gave access to a well, dug beneath the lists, which was always full of water. The Vade Tower resembles the city wall support towers built by the engineers working in the reign of Philip Augustus at Beauvais, Bourges, Chinon (the Coudray Tower), Dourdan, Falaise (the Talbot Tower), Gisors (the Prisoner's Tower), Laon (the King's Tower), Vernon (the Archives Tower)... Like these other towers, the Vade is a real dungeon. It has its own fireplace equipped with bread

Tour de la Vade, Plan 18

An abandoned wall

Along part of the east side, the Gallo-Roman wall, which had been restored by Louis IX, was razed to the ground by Philip III's architects. In its place, but farther forward, they put up much more impressive buildings: the Narbonne Towers, the Trésau Tower, and the curtain as far as the Tower of the Constable's Mill, visible in the background.

oven, its own well and latrines. It has sometimes been compared with the Constance Tower of Aigues-Mortes, which was built at the same time. Here a spiral staircase leads to a gallery built inside the wall surrounding the upper part of the ground floor room. At Carcassonne the staircase was built inside the wall around the rooms it led into, and went right up to the battlement.

It was also probably during the period of construction following the siege of 1240, that most of the residential part of the castle were heightened. The two pseudo-dungeons were raised (Viollet-le-Duc put a Flemish gable on the roof of one of these dungeons, in limitation of the one on the Trésau Tower), and a second storey was added to the lodge perpendicular to the towers.

« Donjons », Plan 7

Tour du Trésau, Plan 2

In 1242 the Cité received its first permanent garrison. The men did not lodge in the castle, but arms and munitions were stocked there. The royal administration and the military command were increased. The addition of an extra storey provided more room.

The important construction works of the late 13th century

For the next twenty-five years (the Vade Tower was completed in 1245), there were no important changes in the Cité fortifications. The next stage of alteration works took place around 1280 in the reign of Philip III. This time it concerned the inner wall which was changed significantly. The whole of the south angle, from the Tower of the Saint-Nazaire Four (formerly known as the Visigoth Tower) to the Saint-Martin Tower, was entirely rebuilt. At the base of the Burlas Tower there is a semi-cylindrical shaft of a Gallo-Roman tower. This shows us that, at least in this spot, the new fortification was built slightly further back than the Later Empire

Tour du Grand Burlas, Plan 15

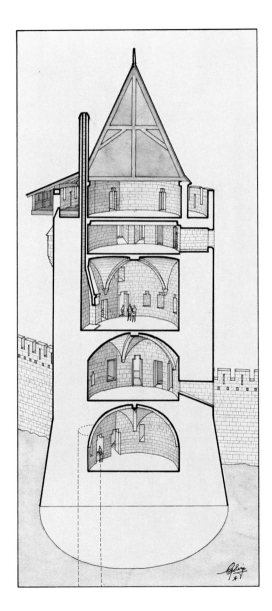

The Vade Tower

It dominates the Saint-Michel swelling and is an independent building with its own wells, fireplace, bread oven and latrines.
Drawing by J.-C. Golvin.

wall, in order to increase the area between the two walls. From the Saint-Martin Tower to the Saint-Sernin Tower, the Gallo-Roman constructions remain the backbone of the fortification, but, as a result of the combination of the under-pining works, the raised sections, the parts of the walls which have been rebuilt, and of the total or partial modifications to the towers, very little of the Later Empire constructions remains visible. The most impressive work carried out during this period was the construction of the Narbonne Towers, the Trésau Tower and the curtain which was brought up to join the Tower of the Constable's Mill. Along this last stretch, the royal architects left behind the Gallo-Roman wall, which had only recently been repaired, after partially pulling it down and burying it. About three quarters of the inner wall was repaired or rebuilt under Philip the Bold.

Porte Narbonnaise, Plan 1
Tour du Trésau, Plan 2
Tour du Moulin du connétable, Plan 3

Display of Capetian power

It is clear that the works were inspired by the concern to reinforce the defences along the Pyrenean frontier. In 1280, the problem of the Spanish kingdoms was at the heart of French foreign policy. We know that the building works had begun by this date. In 1275, the King intervened in the Navarre succession. During the minority of the young Queen Jeanne, the country was occupied and treated like a seneschalchy, in spite of the rebellion of the population. Philip III also interfered in the Castille succession, and in 1276, the French army, which had arrived at Béarn, was only stopped from entering Spain by the onset of the winter season. Finally the victories of Charles of Anjou in Italy profoundly upset the King of Aragon, married to Constance of Hohenstaufen, daughter of Manfred, the leader of the Gibelin party and for a short time King of

Sicily. But the works carried out at Carcassonne at the end of the 13th century, are more than a simple modernisation or reinforcement of the fortifications. They are the affirmation of the wealth and power of the Capetians, which had to be displayed even at the limits of the kingdom. The Narbonne Gate and the Trésau Tower are not defence constructions; they should be seen more as imposing buildings, symbols of sovereignty, intended to impress foreign princes as well as the local populations.

Porte Narbonnaise, Plan 1
Tour du Trésau, Plan 2

The large stones are beautifully finished and the stone bossing makes the constructions of this period easily recognisable. The stones are flat on the edges, but the central part comes out. We do not know whether there was any practical reasoning behind this style of stone-cutting, but it is in any case very characteristic of fortifications built at the end of the 13th century (an example is the wall at Aigues-Mortes, built from 1272 onwards), and at the beginning of the 14th century (the Philip the Bel Tower at Villeneuve-lès-Avignon from 1306). However, this "fashion" did not spread throughout France and the stone-bossed constructions seem to be concentrated in several areas, the South-East, the region around Carcassonne, and, to a lesser extent, the Bourbonnais, Champagne... It has been suggested that the bossing made escalades more difficult because it became problematic to place the ladderes securely against the wall. Others have argued that these projections were intended to break up the stone missiles hurled against the wall. It might be that appearance was more important than any pratical reason; it is certainly true that these buildings give off an impression of power and threatening force.

We find the same principles put into practice at the Count's Castle, only this time on a grander scale: the arrow-slits are

arranged in quincunz fashion at different levels, the defence is split, up by changes in level, towers are used to interrupt the sentry route, which itself is supervised from higher levels in the towers, the towers and curtain walls could be hoarded, lateral flanking was guaranteed. The two city gates which were rebuilt (the Saint-Nazaire Gate in the south and the Narbonne Gate in the east), reproduce the double locking system of the castle entrance with the repeated sequence of machicoulis, crossbeam and heavy wooden doors. The leverage mechanisms of the crossbeams are located in two places, one inside the hall and one on a platform outside. The passage under the central lodge, linked by the Narbonne towers, is, moreover, defended by a pole-axe fixed between the two closure systems. The royal engineers used to the best the

Tour Saint-Nazaire, Plan 16

The Vade Town stairs
Built inside the wall.

Tour
Saint-Nazaire,
Plan 16

differences in level between the town and the lists. The Saint-Nazaire Gate entrance is situated five feet above the lists, making the use of the battering ram impossible. The entrance is on the east side of the tower, forcing the enemy to advance parallel to the wall and to expose the right side of their bodies, unprotected by a shield, to the archers. The winding passage determines the square shape of the tower. It is, in fact, the only square tower except for the Bishop's Tower which is built on the extension of the two walls very near this place. The tower goes across the lists and so can easily block them. In both cases, watch-towers were added on the four corners to avoid any blind angles. There were innovations as well. A number of towers were built with a *bec* or beak, which strengthened the central part and defected blows from the battering rams. The determination to conduct an active defence was so strong that the beaks of the Narbonne towers were pierced with arrow slits on the ground floor, an arrangement which contradicted the normal role played by the beak, ie that of reinforcing the building. But this was done so as to best utilise the crossbow, which was most efficient when used at the height of a man. The alcoves for the archers and the crossbowmen were furnished with benches. The surveillance of the surroundings was carried out from the watch-towers along the roof of the Trésau Tower. The Flemish gable on this

Tour
du Trésau,
Plan 2

tower reminds us that the royal architects probably came from the part of France north of the Loire. The lists on the south-east side were now wide and flat, a real boulevard. The defenders' cavalry could now easily charge the attackers who had managed to get over the outer wall. Moreover, such attackers found themselves under the crossfire of arrows shot

Tour de
la Vade,
Plan 18

from the garrison on the Vade Tower, which was totally independent, and of

those sent by archers stationed in the inner wall tower.

Great care was taken in the organisation of a water supply system. During the previous building campaign, the Vade Tower had been built over a well and a vast cistern located against the outer wall near the Aude Gate. The south front could get its supplies from the well of the Saint-Nazaire cloister or from the one in the rue du Plo (called the little well), and it went round the Saint-Nazaire Gate which was built on a well. One of the Narbonne towers was equipped with a huge cistern and the Trésau Tower was situated very near a well. In fact, the main buildings were designed to be independent defence structures, with their own reserves of food (there was a salting tub in the other tower of the Narbonne Gate), their own fireplace, bread oven, latrines... They had to be capable of resisting, even if another part of the town had been occupied, and thus acting as support positions for the reconquest which was sure to come. The example of 1240 had shown that royal reinforcements would never be long in arriving.

Porte d'Aude,
Plan 11

Size and strength of the Cité garrison

Viollet-le-Duc had an excellent grasp of the principles of medieval military architecture, and fully realised that the 13th century, with the supreme example of such architecture in Carcassonne, had been a turning point. He wrote: ''Until the 13th century, defence fortification relied on the mass and position of buildings...'', but he added: ''Afterwards, a new system of fortification was adopted, giving to defence the same active role as that used in attack[15].'' The famous architect took this opinion a bit far perhaps, when he suggested that the defence strategy of confronting the enemy involved maintaining a considerable garrison within the

The south part of the Lists

The Lists were an open space where the enemy could not manœuvre but could be charged. The changes in level on the inner wall guard route and the towers along the wall meant that the defence could be broken up.

walls. He calculated that there was a man behind each arrow slit at Carcassonne, and in this way estimated a total of 1,323 soldiers. The reasoning behind fortifications had always been to economise on manpower. The figures we have for 13th century castle garrisons, for example those described in the royal accounts, seem to us extremely small. These garrisons consisted of a few sergeants ''assisted'' by a pack of dogs, and in the more important castles a few dozen soldiers. When he heard of the rebellion led by Trencavel, Wiliam of Ormes appealed to the knights of the viscounty to join the small troup he had at his disposal.

The lords of French origin who had replaced the *''faidits''* responded positively, but the local nobility were less favourable and some even went over to the enemy. This episode revealed the weakness of the old system of *estage* which went back to the time of the Trencavels. Under this system, the knights owed three months service in the Cité, in return for their fiefs. Each knight, together with his men, was responsible for the defence of one or two towers and a part of the wall.

In 1242, the Cité was sent a permanent garrison of paid soldiers under a constable. This was done to increase the rather un-

The Saint-Nazaire Gate
The side entrance forced the enemy to go along the wall and expose their right side, unprotected by shields, to the defenders' arrows.

reliable feudal levy (in 1268, 25 out of the 42 feudal lords responded to the Seneschal's appeals, and this only after several requests had been made). A payroll of 1260 mentions sixty names. Was this the total force? 200 soldiers are mentioned in a document written in the 14th century, and by the end of the Middle Ages the garrison counted 109 men. In addition to these sergeants, who were mostly crossbowmen, there were the people responsible for the maintenance of the fortification, the master mason, the master carpenter and the workforce under them. We should also include the *artilliator* or specialist in war machines. As early as 1210, Simon de Montfort had mangonels and missile-hurling machines constructed and stored in the Cité. These war machines were used in the sieges undertaken by Montfort (for example at Termes). Unfortunately we know little about the number and kind of war machines stored in the Cité.

The only text we have is an inventory of the royal carpenters drawn up in 1298, but it is little more than a list of spare parts: ropes, bolts, wooden rods, slings, leather thongs, winches, lead plates for the counterweights, wheels, axles, containers for collecting water, tools, millstones, tents and poles for the tournaments... We have a little more information about the arms, which seem to have been stored in quantity. In 1277, 46 cases of arrows and about fifty crossbows were taken from the arsenal and sent to Pampelune. In 1288, the King of Majorca was ''lent'' fifty cases of crossbow quarrels, in 1324 several hundred crossbows of different types were sent to Agenais, together with the corresponding quarrels, and in 1345 three dozen siege slings and their accessories... So we see that by the end of the 13th century (the important construction works of Philip the Bold were probably completed shortly

after his death), the Cité had become an exceptional fortress, because of its permanent garrison and because of the arms guarded there. The fortifications were so impressive that during the Hundred Years War the Cité was never attacked.

The Saint-Nazaire Gate

A right-angled entrance, two separate systems of portcullis, machicoulis and gates. But also a well, a fireplace and a bread oven for the south gate of the inner wall. Drawing by J.-C. Golvin.

TOWN OR FORTRESS?

Throughout the Later Middle Ages the Cité was a permanently guarded fortress. Every evening, thirty-eight conscripted men-at-arms and trumpeters were posted on the curtain walls and the inner wall towers, or at the Narbonne Gate, or they were sent to patrol the lists. During the day, twenty or so heavily-armed sergeants, dressed in the *camail* or hood of mail, and wearing a sword, controlled strangers who came to the Narbonne Gate. Such outsiders had to "say with whom they had business and leave their arms at the gate".

Porte Narbonnaise, Plan 1

Security promotes economic development, too many precautions stifle it. The new town, which, after several abortive attempts, had been founded on the west bank of the Aude in 1262, was only surrounded by a rough-and-ready rammed earth wall, except in the west, where there was a stone wall which also served as a dyke against the river; yet it had quickly attracted most of the manufacturing and commercial activities, and had become one of the most important cloth-manufacturing centres in the South. In 1304 there were, 2,300 families in the town, making a total population of 10,000 according to Jean-Marie Carbasse[16]. It was now a real town, rather than just the bourg of the Cité, and was probably already built on the checker-board plan that we know today, since it is so characteristic of the bastides or free cities which were springing up in royal Languedoc at this period. However, the Cité was much more than just a fortress, more than a garrison town and rallying point for the local nobility when they were commanded to assemble *"en chevaux et en armes"*

Ville basse, Plan 24

(with horses and arms) to serve the king. It was also an important administrative and religious centre. Alongside the Seneschal, who was responsible for the maintenace of law and order, there were the lawyers, notaries, prosecutors, auditors, provosts, lieutenants and civil sergeants. The latter were notorious for their excessive greed and corruption, and were called *comestores* (devourers). The Trésau (treasury) Tower housed the tax offices. The Knights Hall, which took up the whole of the second floor of the Narbonne Gate block, was more a state room than a place of defence. In the second half of the 13th century a huge audience hall supported by pillars was built on the spot now occupied by the Midi Courtyard. A Gothic window cut into the raised curtain wall provided the necessary lighting, and the room was heated from a fireplace still visible today. The hall may have been used for the assemblies of the Seneschalchy Estates; when they had their first assembly in 1269, the vast residence of Gui de Levis, one of the king's vassals, was too small for their needs. The hall disappeared in the 15th century, when alterations were made to the administration and law offices.

Tour du Trésau, Plan 2

The bishop and chapter had regained their former prestige and authority and the Inquisition was extremely active. In times of peace, the prelate had the use of the rooms in the Bishop's Tower, and of the round tower, which was sometimes called the Inquisition Tower. Both of these towers were situated near the Bishop's Palace. It would seem that the lower room of the Inquisition Tower was designed to be used as a prison.

Tour carrée de l'Evêque, Plan 14

Tour de l'Inquisition, Plan 13

Plot against the Inquisition

Tour de la Justice, Plan 10

The Inquisition archives and registers were most probably stored in the Justice Tower. In 1283, these documents were at the centre of a strange plot[17]. They contained information on individuals, denunciations and declarations made against others. The mystery surrounding these documents created an atmosphere of deep anxiety. A small group of the leading citizens of Carcassonne approached a certain Bernard Lagarrigue, a servant of the Inquisitor Jean Galand, and asked him to obtain the documents for them. Everything was ready and Lagarrique had already been handsomely paid, when he suddenly admitted that he could not read and that he might therefore steal the wrong papers. The notables found a professional copyist named Bernard Agasse to help him, but by this time Jean Galand had probably got wind of the affair. He had left for Toulouse with the key of the archives room, and denounced one of the main plotters, Sans Morlane, Archdeacon of the

The Cité, seen from the Pinte Tower
*The central building and the castle gate towers, the semi-circular barbican
and, at the other end of the town, the back of the Narbonne Gate and of the Trésau Tower.*

The Trésau Tower

*An enormous unit of defence, and also the head-
quarters of financial administration. A vast
fireplace and latrines contributed to the comfort
of the royal officers. Drawing by J.-C. Golvin.*

The Justice Tower

*The Inquisition archives were probably stored in
this tower (centre of the photo).*

church of Sainte-Marie-du-Bourg-Neuf, to
Pope Honorius III. The Pope rejected the
accusation and reproached the inquisitor
for using irregular procedures.

Out of hatred for the Inquisition, the
people of Carcassonne turned for the last
time to Spain. In 1303, the Franciscan,
Bernard Delicieux, and the leading
citizens of the town, had succeeded in ar-
ranging for inspectors to visit the town in
order to temper the enthusiasm of the
Dominicans. In February 1304, Philip the
Bel was enthusiastically welcomed at Carcassonne. Encouraged by the previous
success against the Dominicans, a burgess
addressed the King with perhaps a little
too much vehemence and demanded
justice against the Inquisition. The King
had him put aside without a word.

Was the attitude of the King considered
unfavourable? In the following months,
Bernard Delicieux, the consul Elie Patrice
(known as the "little King" in the new
town) and a groupe of notables offered
their services to Ferrant, Infanta of Majorca and son of the King of Aragon, and suggested that he lead a rebellion in the Languedoc. King James informed Philip the
Bel. No mercy was shown to the guilty.
Elie Patrice, along with eight consuls and
burgesses, was hanged, Bernard Delicieux
was imprisoned and the bourg was fined
the large sum of 60,000 livres, (Bernard
Lagarrigue and Bernard Agasse had
received 200 livres for their aborted break-
in). The bourg was also deprived of its
consulate and thus lost its administrative
autonomy. However, in 1307, two years
after his final anti-French movement, the
King granted the town a pardon.

The fight against heresy was not just
repressive; it had its positive aspects. The
reconstruction of the choir and transept
of the Saint-Nazaire Cathedral and the
erection of two big churches in the Lower Town bear witness to the desire for a
renewed faith which inspired the clergy.

Eglise
Saint-Nazaire,
Plan 17

Les Emmurés de Carcassonne
This painting by Jean-Paul Laurens, known for his big historical
compositions, portrays Bernard Delicieux delivering the victims of the
Inquisition. The artist used the word emmuré (walled up/prisoner) in its
modern sense. The mur (wall) or mure stands for prison. At Carcassonne
the prison had a little garden. Musée du Luxembourg.

But the solutions adopted in the Cité and the new bourg were completely different.

The churches of the Lower Town

Two churches were built in the Lower Town, in the parish of Saint-Michel and Saint-Vincent. Like the two bourgs, which had previously flanked the Cité, they were built to the north and south of the Cité. It soon became clear that the churches were too small. The construction of the *Eglise Saint-Michel, Plan 25* church of Saint-Michel was begun in 1283, but we do not know exactly when it was finished. Work was interrupted at the beginning of the 14th century and was then recommenced, this time using different building materials. It has been so altered and the restorations of Viollet-le-Duc were so radical that, as Marcel Durliat says in his masterly study, it is now "essentially a 19th century building". However, this building has a number of features in common with those of the churches built in the same period by the monastic orders. The ground plan is very simple, consisting of one wide nave (with no transept or side aisles) and a central apse flanked by two apsidioles. Only the side chapels and the three aspses had ribbed vaults originally. Diaphragm arches supported the nave. As a result of the windows that Viollet-le-Duc had put in, the church is today much lighter than it was originally.

The construction of the church of Saint-Vincent was begun in 1308 on the same plan. The nave, which is a little wider, was not vaulted until much later, towards the second half of the 18th century (the Saint-Michel vaults were probably added at the end of the 17th century and the beginning of the 18th century). Here, also, only a little light penetrates. This kind of church was to become very popular in the Aude, satisfying, undoubtedly, the need for vast, bare spaces to accomodate the greatest possible number, and to help preach reconquest in a region where anticlericalism and heresy had far from disappeared.

The reconstruction of the Saint-Nazaire choir and transept

The principles underlying the partial reconstruction of the cathedral of Saint-Nazaire were quite different. In 1096, just *Eglise Saint-Nazaire, Plan 17* after the construction of the Romanesque cathedral had begun, Pope Urban II had blessed the stones of the future cathedral. The church, which replaced a Carolingian building, was completed in about 1130. Work began again just a century later. At the end of 1269, the bishop and chapter were given authority to push back the road, running alongside the cathedral choir, by two *cannes* (about twelve feet). The transept and the choir could now be reconstructed. What was behind such an undertaking? The church does not seem to have suffered in the fighting of 1209 and 1240. In 1209, according to Peter of Vaux-de-Cernay, "in order to reinforce the city walls, the inhabitants, perverse people without faith, had demolished the refectory and the canons' storeroom and, even more terrible, the church stalls". This can probably be explained by the need for wood, always in great demand on the part of the defenders. The uncle of the chronicler, the new Bishop of Carcassonne, began the work of repairing the damage as early as 1215, and twenty years later there was no trace of the "sacrilege". The declared intention of enlarging the cathedral was probably sincere; very little was gained in length, but the transept took on proportions that it certainly did not have in the Romanesque building. Did that justify the considerable financial effort engaged? The bishops devoted a large portion of their revenue to the effort, will donations were asked for, appeals made to the faithful, indulgences promised to generous donors for a certain number of specified faults ranging from lack of respect towards parents through to minor acts of plundering and usury, and finally the whole clergy of the diocese was mobilised. The reconstruction of the choir and the transept symbolised the reaction to heresy and the adhesion to Capetian France, as well as being the simple enlarging of a church. This was the Church's way of replying to the ascetism of the ''perfects'' and their refusal of wordly things. The restored cathedral represented the beauty of human achievements in the service of Faith. The Church had been accused of losing its influence. The Abbot Jean Rocacher used the example of the decoration on the reconstructed parts of the cathedral to refute such criticisms, arguing that the Church's influence was ''emphasised through the symbols and images of its earthly roots[19]''. A sanctuary which took its inspiration from that most dazzling of royal constructions, the Sainte-Chapelle of Paris, was offered to those who were reticent in their feelings concerning the annexation to the royal domain.

After 1248, the prelates of the Crusade, Gui of Vaux-de-Cernay, then Clarin, formerly Montfort's chaplain, were succeeded by local men of great personal character. William Razouls (or Radulphe) must have been a man of extraordinary ablility; this child of a family of serfs from Trebes was admitted as a student by the chapter. In 1223 his friends clubbed together to pay for his liberty. He became principal archdeacon, and then bishop in 1255. In 1259, he had the chapter infirmary chapel reconstructed. This was to be the first Gothic construction built in Carcassonne

and it was probably at this moment that the idea of rebuilding the transept of the cathedral took root. The work was begun under William Radulphe's successor, Bernard of Capendu, a young man less than thirty years old. His ''insufficient knowledge'' (that is of university grades), which worried the Curia at Rome, was compensated for by his daring, his dynamism and his determination to administer the diocese with rigour. Finding themselves in the middle of a reformed and revitalised Church and in the service of a royal administration for which they would become the best technicians, the local elite turned their backs on heresy and became the most ardent artisans of unification.

The Romanesque nave

Both Viollet-le-Duc and Mérimée recognised the originality of the half-Romanesque half-Gothic cathedral of Saint-Nazaire. The two styles are profoundly different, yet the juxtaposition in this building is harmonious. The Romanesque construction gives an impression of hierarchy of volumes and balance. The fairly wide nave is flanked by two narrow side aisles with semicircular barrel vaults reaching up to the central pointed barrel vault. These thus provide perfectly balanced support for the central barrel vault but meant that it was not possible to insert windows high up. The little light that there is comes from the lower windows of the side aisles and from three open *oculi* in the west wall in alignment with the three aisles. The vaults spring up from the capitals of a series of pillars. Massive cylindrical pillars alternate with square pillars which have embedded

Eglise Saint-Nazaire, Plan 17

The church of Saint-Nazaire
In the foreground, the remains of the chapter-house, further back, the Radulphe chapel, in the background, the south arm of the transept.

columns on each side. The transverse ribs of the nave and the side aisles rest slightly higher up either on short half columns starting from the capitals of the circular pillars, or on the embedded columns of the pillars extended up to this level. The capitals are decorated with leaf-work, fighting animals and geometric designs, all carved in a very pure style with references to Antiquity, but there is nothing particularly original in the work.

A masterpiece of radiant Gothic

When we look at the plan of the reconstruction of the choir and transept, certain details, like the square pillars flanked with half columns at the crossing, reminiscent of the nave, lead us to think that, from the very beginning, the intention was to make only a partial reconstruction and to give a coherent style to the church, while leaving the two contrasting styles side by side. The architects working at the end of the 13th century and the beginning

of the 14th, showed remarkable skill in adapting to the lack of space in the east, and in constructing the verticals in such a way that the extended nave did not seem out of proportion. They also managed to let in a lot of light. It was not possible to build an ambulatory, so the apse was reserved for the clergy. It consists of seven stained glass windows, the lower parts of which have a light stonework support. On the east of each arm of the transept there is a narrow side aisle. Here the vaults reach up to the same level and act as a buttress to the transept vaults, rendering the use of buttresses unnecessary on the exterior. In the alignment of the Romanesque nave, the choir bay interrupts this side aisle. The six chapels with flat apses connected by the side aisle serve as apsidal chapels. As in the apse itself, there are huge windows at the end of these chapels, resting on a low wall support. Altogether, the effect achieved is that of a vast wall of light, which the virtual lack of any partitioning makes even more spectacular. The walls separating the chapels only go up as far as the base of the windows; after this they become open-work bays using the same design as that of the tracery. The vaults go up as high as those of the side aisle and the transept. At the north and south ends of the transept, two big rose windows bring in side lighting.

There were a number of technical problems involved in bringing all the vaults to the same height. To cancel out the unequal parts, iron braces were stretched between the tops of the pillars and the beginnings of the vaults. The effect is not particularly aesthetic. A more successful innovation was achieved by let-

A wheel crane
One of the leverage techniques probably used in the construction of the transept and choir of Saint-Nazaire. Drawing by J.-C. Golvin, from a manuscript in the Pierpont Morgan Library.

The Saint-Nazaire transept and choir
The entire east end of the church is nothing less than a wall of light. The emphasis on lightness and balance made necessary the use of rather ugly iron struts.

ting some of the arches go down into their supports, giving the support columns a slim, graceful appearance. These ''penetrating arches'' which merged directly with the pillar and did not rest on a capital, became a characteristic element of ''flamboyant'' Gothic. Two of the three decorative elements, the stained glass windows and the sculptures, are sufficiently well preserved for us to judge their quality. Very little remains of the third element, that of the paintings which decorate the walls and the vaults. It is only on the choir vaults that we can still distinguish the painting of a Christ in glory, angels and symbols of the evangelists. The polychromy was fairly bold, with blues, reds, purple, yellow and ochre.

The stained glass windows

The remaining windows are among the most beautiful of the South. Unfortunately, the whole effect is slightly spoilt by the windows dating from the beginning of the 16th century. These let in too much light, and have large scale compositions which interrupt the beautiful silver work of the Gothic windows... The iconography of the medieval windows in the apse follows traditional themes. The life of Christ is depicted in the centre, that of Saint Peter and Saint Paul on the left, and on the right we see the life of Saint Nazaire and Saint Celse, the patron saints of the church. The themes treated in the two remaining windows of the transept, are more original. In the first chapel of the north-east arm we have the tree of Jesse. The tree, bearing the ancestors of the Virgin Mary and of Christ, springs from Jesse who lies along the bottom of the window in the centre. The prophets announcing the coming of the Messiah are lined up on both sides. The tree of life in the first chapel of the south arm illustrates a text of Saint Bonaventura. This Franciscan, a

professor of theology at Paris in the middle of the 13th century, suggested in a poetic and erudite meditation that the virtues and good deeds of the Saviour should be arranged as the fruits of the tree of life, a tree which also produced the wood of the Holy Cross. The artists working at the end of the 13th century and the beginning of the 14th century were attracted by this image, and we see it also, for example, in the fresco by Taddeo Gaddi in the Santa Croce in Florence, although the Italian work is undoubtedly later than the Saint-Nazaire window. A big, perfectly circular rose window, dedicated to the Virgin Mary adorns the north wall. As Marcel Durliat points out[20], ''one really has the impression that the window is turning. The decoration of blind arcades on the wall below the window is deliberately asymetrical, with the left side going up higher than the right side, and this seems to set the whole thing in motion''. The colours are fairly dark, red, blue, green, with yellow used mainly in the trefoils separating the petal ends. The design of the south rose window is more complex: in the centre a quatrefoil shows Christ seated in majesty, with the surrounding twelve petals forming a first corolla, the petals then divide into two and end in a point with a quatrefoil. The decision to pierce the upper part of the wall, and the regularity of the blind arcades on the lower part, give a static appearance to the central wheel, in contrast to that obtained on the north wall. The colours are very light, with a predominance of yellow and emerald. In the two quatrefoils at the base of the rose window we see the arms of the Bishop Peter of Rochefort (1301-1321). This enables us to date the completion of the reconstruction works to the beginning of the 14th century. The work began in the apse, continued with the construction of the north arm of the transept and finished in the south.

The North Rose Window
*The North Rose Window dedicated to Mary, together with the South Rose
Window dedicated to Christ, and the medieval stained glass windows
in the apse and in the arms of the transept constitute the finest set
of stained glass windows in the Midi.*

A local school of sculpture with northern influence

The sculpted decoration reveals both the influence of the art of the French court and the evolution of a local school of sculpture which managed to retain its personality.

The first work of importance is the tomb of Bishop Radulphe, discovered in 1839, when the chapel was cleared of the mounds of earth which had accumulated there. The bishop, who died in 1266, is represented in bas-relief on a flagstone fixed to the west wall of the chapel. There is little expression in the face and the clothing falls in a fairly mechanical way, but the embroidery on the alb and chasuble, and the fringes of the stole are delicately wrought. As Michèle Pradalier-Schlumberger says[21], this type of flat tomb fixed against a wall shows no sign of northern influence, and its origin can probably be traced more accurately to the Roussillon region. A sarcophagus is embedded underneath the flagstone. The top part of the sarcophagus is decorated with finely executed foliage. Beneath this, there is an inscription recounting the construction of the chapel, the virtuous old age of Radulphe, and his eleven years as bishop. The lower part of the sarcophagus is devoted to a funeral scene. The centre part of this scene, showing the ceremony of absolution, is represented with a fair degree of realism — the dead man's soul, in the form of a small child, is seen going up to heaven. The dead man himself is surrounded by the officiating priests (including a bishop), and what might be his sister and nephew. The funeral procession of the canons, is, in contrast, extremely monotonous, and reveals an awkward copying of the northern style. This type of funeral decoration, in which we see people standing beneath arches mourning the dead man, was to rapidly replace the tomb stones with incised work, exemplified by the one that now hangs on the west wall of the south arm of the transept, and which may have originally covered the tomb of Simon de Montfort, before his remains were taken away by his son.

Most of the decoration in the apse has been restored. According to the baron Guilhermy, who visited the site on a number of occasions, ''only a few vestiges and broken pieces of statue remained. Perrin the sculptor made a good job of restoring them''. It is difficult to know how rigorous Perrin was, or how much he improvised, but whatever the case, his sculptures are full of life and charm. The twenty-two statues decorating the pillars in the choir are reminiscent of the Sainte-Chapelle in Paris. Although there is clear influence from outside, the execution is different here. The Saint-Nazaire statues were carved out of the same block of stone as the pillars, while the pillars were being built, whereas in the Sainte-Chapelle in Paris the statues are separate entities added to the pillars. The style is pure Carcassonnais and is in no way a servile imitation of northern sculpture. The heads are fairly small, with prominent, wide-open eyes, drawn up towards the temples. The wavy hair is brushed back leaving the forehead clear. The folds of the clothes are clearly shown by means of vertical and oblique lines. Broken lines are used to suggest the sagging of the clothes in those places where they are fixed loosely. It is not possible to identify all the statues. Of the twelve apostles, some remain anonymous. We recognise the patron saints of the church, Nazaire with his hair plastered back, revealing a high forehead, and with his prominent cheekbones and very expressive lips, and Celse with his smiling, baby face. We can also recognise Saint Gimer, one of the town's first bishops. There is a statue of the Virgin Mary holding her infant a little away from her; she leans over and looks down pensively at the baby, who strokes his mother's chin and tries to attract her attention.

The statues were not all made by the same hand. Some are stiff, the faces of the apostles are stereotyped, and the gestures are awkward. Others are much more graceful, with flowing lines, and individual, expressive faces. The style evolves and becomes more refined as time passes and the works progress from the choir towards the transept.

This evolution reached its apogee in the tomb of Bishop Peter of Rochefort, situated in the chapel he had built in the northeast part of the Romanesque nave. The chapel was finished by the time the bishop died in 1321. To a certain extent, the funeral monument uses the techniques of the Radulphe tomb, but the interpretation is freer and perfectly executed. The bishop stands out from the wall in round relief, and this gives the statue life. The act of benediction is perfectly and realistically achieved, and there is nothing rigid or stiff in the facial expression. An archdeacon stands on each side of the bishop. Below, there is no imitation sarcophagus, and the lower section merges into the upper part of the triptych. The funeral procession with its mourners standing under the arches, provides an opportunity for the artist to exercise his style. The faces are all fairly similar, but there is a great deal of variety in the attitudes, the body postures, the treatment of clothing and accessories.

A partially successful restoration

The outside of the church is disappointing, and Viollet-le-Duc's restoration work is in part responsible for this. Inside the church, the cleaning of the walls and the numerous restoration works (paving, pil-

Bishop Peter of Rochefort
«The apogee of what is most personal and most provincial in the cathedral's sculpture»
(Michèle Pradalier-Schlumberger).

lars, window tracery) were on the whole successful. The restoration of the stained glass windows, carried out by the Parisian artist Gérente, is at times controversial, and he himself admitted that he had done "what he could". But in general, the place was saved from ruin, without being at all spoilt. The same can not be said of the exterior. The decoration, the balustrades, the capping of the stair turrets, the crenellation of the west wall, carried out because Viollet-le-Duc was convinced that the Later Empire wall, which he thought was "Visigothic", came as near as possible to the church at this point, all these restorations added nothing to the monument. Quite the contrary. Viollet-le-Duc, moreover, was not lucky. He wrote: "The grain of the stone I am going to use is similar to the grain of the original stone, but it is far superior in quality." If we judge by the present state of certain pinnacles and gables, the stone has resisted no better than the original.

The beginnings of rivalry between the Cité and the Lower Town

At the beginning of the 14th century, the Cité was a town with imposing buildings, reflecting its strategic, administrative and religious importance. The diocese was not big, yet a number of important figures were nominated to head it, like Peter of the Taillefer Chapel (1291-1298), a former canon of Paris, who was asked to collect the necessary funds for the Aragon Crusade, and later became Cardinal. Another example was Jean of Chevry (1298-1300), a former archdeacon of Reims and a famous jurist. Peter of Rochefort (1300-1321) was a local man who probably had a considerable personal fortune; his arms can be seen on the many buildings he had constructed (the key of the sexpartite vault of the choir and the south rose window in the church of Saint-Nazaire, the church of Rouffiac, the church of Fanties d'Aude...) both in the Cité and in the surrounding villages. Peter

Eglise
Saint-Nazaire,
Plan 17

Rodier (1323-1330) was canon of Paris, then secretary, and later chancellor to Philip V, before becoming bishop of Carcassonne.

As the seat of a seneschalchy covering more than 120 kilometres from north to south and 70 to 150 kilometres from east to west, the Cité was the political and legal centre of a territory which went well beyond the present borders of the Aude department. In 1303, 117 royal sergeants working in the provost's office, the castellany and the *baillage* (bailiff's court) made up the basic personnel of the civil administration. In 1314 the number had gone up to 142, and in addition there were the "local sergeants" whose responsibility only extended to the towns where they lived[22]. All these people who ruled and policed the country under the authority of the provosts and bailiffs, were nominated by the seneschal and could be dismissed or moved by him at any moment. Last but not least, the Cité was a fortress. During one of the expeditions of the

Hundred Years War, led by the Black Prince in the autumn of 1355, the Lower Town was taken in spite of the heroic resistance of some of the inhabitants. Most of the population took refuge behind the walls of the Cité, and the massive defences stopped the English from going further. Safe behind the walls, the notables of the bourg tried to negotiate and offered a large sum in return for leaving their town intact. But Edward III's son refused to negotiate and the bourg was pillaged and then burnt to the ground. The Black Prince, who got his name from the colour of his armour pressed on to Narbonne, where he was only able to take the bourg. When he came to the "sea of Greece" (the Mediterranean) he turned round and went back to Guyenne. The episode reveals the important role played by the urban fortifications when they

The South-West Front
Standing out from the fields and vineyards, the Cité seems here to be turning its back on its rival, the Lower Town.

were sufficiently powerful. They diverted the problems onto the surrounding countryside and those towns which were less protected, they prevented any lasting occupation of the area and reduced most of the military expeditions to *"chevauchées"*, which gave little political advantage. The Seneschal, Thibaut of Barbazan, learnt from this episode and in the following weeks, had the towns, cities and castles inspected "and fortified those places which could be defended". The ransom offered by the inhabitants for their Lower Town (250,000 gold *écus*, according to the probably exaggerated estimation of certain chroniclers), indicates how wealthy the bourg was, in spite of the plague which had spread desolation several years previously. This prosperity was mainly due to the wool trade (the bourg had taken the Easter lamb as its emblem) and the cloth trade. And this was the great weakness of the Cité: it had no economic activity to speak of. In this respect, the Cité was no longer a self-sufficient town; on the other side of the Aude, the bourg had its own quasi-autonomous existence, with its consuls, and its councils of notables. The Lower Town was entirely rebuilt following the fire of 1355, which only

Ville basse, Plan 24

L'Aude, Plan 23

South corner of the Cité
Between the Justice Tower (in the foreground) and the church of Saint-Nazaire (in the background), a space formerly occupied by the Bishop's Palace and the Canons' Enclosure.

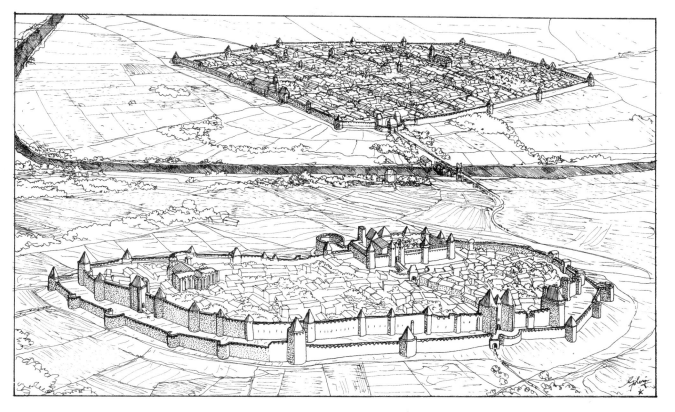

spared the churches. The town was now spread over a smaller area, but was protected by a stone wall, flanked with small semi-circular towers and with a trench in front. Manufacturing activities and trade, the two essential elements of urban life, started up again. But the Cité, closed in by its walls, and proud of its military and administrative role, could not, and did not want to incorporate these elements into its own life. In 1420, 1421, and 1423, the

Languedoc States met at Carcassonne to swear loyalty to the Dauphin Charles, who became King Charles VII in 1422, and to discuss the subsidies which the province was ready to give the Prince and then the new King in his fight against the English. But the Estates held council in the bourg, as though the Cité was no longer the heart of one of the ''good towns'' of the kingdom, but simply a fortress a little off the beaten track.

The Cité and the Lower Town
The fortress and the linen manufacturing town separated by the Aude.
Drawing by J.-C. Golvin.

AN UNUSUAL FATE

There were many reasons for the decline. In fact, the walls and towers benefitted from a sort of "progressive disinterest". This disinterest did not save the monument from falling into ruin, but it did mean that until the Revolution, unlike other fortifications, the Cité was not destroyed or irremediably changed, in the name of progress or expediency.

By the beginning of the 14th century, the Crown had won over the people of Languedoc. In this loyal country, the king's men no longer really needed military support. However, since the Hundred Years War had not finished, and the frontier with Aragon was not far off, the Cité retained its strategic role. It was the central element of a defence system which, in 1483, was described in the following way: "On the Aragonese frontier there is the Cité of Carcassonne, the mother, with her five sons, Puylaurens, Aguilar, Quierbus, Pierrepertuse and Termes... and all the guards of these castles may be called frontier troops[23]". The moments of tension were, however, rare and shortlived. The intrigues of Louis XI in Spain ended with the occupation of the Roussillon after two years of "bitter and cruel war", and pushed back the borders of the kingdom for the first time. The troops were put on the alert again when Charles VIII restored the Roussillon and Cerdagne to Ferdinand of Aragon, and as a result of the rivalry between Ferdinand's grandson, Charles V, and François I. In 1536 the King assured his subjects that *"nous vous avons bien vouluz advertir du bon grant ordre et provision que nous avons donne en toutes les frontieres, entrees et passaiges de nostre royaulme..."* (We wanted to advise you of the good order and provision that we have organised on all the frontiers, entry points and routes of our kingdom.) Arms were accumulated in the Cité... paid for by the municipality. The Spanish troops stopped "their crafty and damned projects". In return for the role it played in defending the kingdom, the Cité was granted a number of priveleges, including tax exemptions for the sergeants and inhabitants of the Cité. On the eve of the Revolution, the *cahiers de doléances* of Carcassonne show that the sergeants and inhabitants were still claiming "immunity from the taille and all ordinary and extraordinary taxes", as granted to them by Saint Louis. By the 14th century the profession of sergeant-crossbowman had become hereditary. By the middle of the 16th century the pay for this profession was 22 *livres* and 15 *sous* per year, payable in three instalments, on Saint Aubin's, on All Souls Day and on Saint John the Baptist's Day. This was not a large sum, but in addition, the men received a certain amount of free salt, and best of all, they had enough free time between guard duty days to allow them to take on another job.

The garrison, now reduced to 110 men, included wool carders, a registrar, an innkeeper, embroiderers, dressmakers, a school teacher, drapers, weavers, a locksmith, stone-masons... all proud of being *"morte-payes"*, a term indicating the hereditary nature of their trade and the priveleges they enjoyed. As part of Richelieu's campaign to stop the Hapsburgs from dominating Europe, a long war broke out between France and Spain in 1635. The Spanish offensive came from Flanders, and most of the fighting took place in northern France. But when the

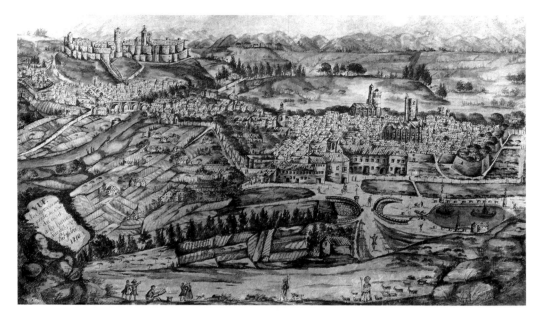

The two Carcassonne in 1840

In the foreground, the Midi canal lock. The Lower Town has lost its walls,
but the corner bastions remain. The Cité gives the impression of being "off-centre".

Catalans rebelled against the administration of Philip IV, France was able to reconquer the Roussillon and in 1642, Louis XIII took Perpignan. The war contined until 1659, but hardly concerned the South. It finally came to an end with the so-called Treaty of the Pyrénées, which confirmed the annexation of the Roussillon and the Cerdagne. With the marriage of Louis XIV to the Infanta of Spain and the confirmation of the new frontier between the two countries, the Cité lost its role of frontier fortress for good.

And time stood still

From a technical point of view, the fortifications were very out of date. Gunpowder artillery began to appear in the second half of the 14th century, but for many years the new canons did not influence military architects, who continued to build as they had done in the past. At first, the canons forged out of cast iron, were fragile, and the stone balls they projected easily broke against the walls. The powder charge was sometimes reduced, in order to prevent the whole thing from breaking up, but this also reduced the range and power of the canons, or sometimes the calibre was increased, but this made the canons so heavy that they became difficult to use.

It was only at the end of the 15th century, that military architecture began to change in a significant way, when harder, metal balls and bronze canons began to be used generally. But Carcassonne continued to rely on the protection provided by its double walls. A few round holes for firing guns were pierced beneath the arrow-slits, and the odd platform was installed for mortars. From time to time, when confronted with a badly equipped

army, the fortifications continued to fulfil their role, during the Wars of Religion for example, or more recently, at the end of the Second World War. In March 1944, the German High Commander of the occupation troops became concerned about the increasing resistance activities in the maquis of the Corbières and the Black Mountains, and requisitioned the Cité. The inhabitants were given eight days to leave their homes and find refuge in the Lower Town. A company occupied the finest of the residences and hotels, the other houses were left vacant and the castle became a munitions depot. The entrances to the town were walled up, except for the Narbonne Gate which was given a heavy wooden door and put under permanent guard. Until August 1944, the Cité thus became a fortress once again, taking on a role which had been long since forgotten. From the reign of Louis XIV the walled Cité had lost its strategic importance and could no more be counted on for defence; as a result, it no longer interested the monarchy. The fate of the Cité was no longer linked, as it had been since 1226, with that of the kingdom. At the same period, the balance between the two Carcassonne was also broken. Faced with the increasing prosperity of its former bourg, the Cité had at least been able to pride itself on its administrative and religious role. But then the Bishop and most of the royal officers left the Cité for the Lower Town. In 1657 by an order of the

Porte Narbonnaise, Plan 1

The Cross-Mayrevieille Road, at the beginning of the 20th century
The passage between the two towers of the Narbonne Gate and the way up to the castle.

Ville basse, Plan 24

King's council, "the headquarters and consistory of the seneschal and the Carcassonne presidial were transferred from the place of the Cité in the High Town to the Lower Town". The reasons given to justify this decision were that the Cité was "on a mountain situated at a fair distance from the Lower Town where the magistrates and officers had their homes", and that "the bad roads made it difficult to reach the Cité in bad weather". In 1801 the church of Saint-Michel replaced the church of Saint-Nazaire as cathedral. But the prelates had not waited for this to happen to take up residence in the Lower Town, only venturing up to the Cité for Lent. The Cité, deserted by its notables and left to the poor, became no more than

Eglise Saint-Michel, Plan 25

Eglise Saint-Nazaire, Plan 17

a suburb of Carcassonne. Poverty was soon to freeze it in a forgotten past. In 1837 Stendhal wrote: "I go up to this ancient town... no sign of civilisation... and I suddenly realise that I am in the middle of the 15th century town."

Tourism and the revival of interest in the monument are two of the main elements of the Carcassonne economy. In this way, the Cité's destiny is once again linked with the central administration of the country, which controls this unique architectural ensemble and does its best to welcome as many visitors as possible to a place originally designed to keep people out. A strange destiny for this town become suburb, for this fortress become historical monument.

Beginnings of tourism
Use of the great hall of the Count's Castle as reception hall (about 1920).

NOTES

1. Although Louis-Napoléon was interested in the Middle Ages and in military affairs, he did not consider this visit an archeological one, seeing it rather in purely political terms. The crowd welcomed him with cries of *"Vive l'Empereur"*, a still strictly illegal acclamation. Five days later he was to utter the famous "Empire is peace". He was entirely absorbed by preparations for the plebiscite of 21st/22nd November 1852, concerning the restoration of the Empire. It is also hardly likely that the author of *The Abolition of pauperism* would have wished to be confronted with the sight of the impoverished inhabitants of the Cité.

2. Marcel Durliat "L'ancienne cathédrale Saint-Nazaire de Carcassonne", in *Congrès archéologique de France*, 181st session, 1973, Pays d'Aude.

3. Elie Griffe, *les Anciens Pays de l'Aude dans l'Antiquité et au Moyen Âge*, Carcassonne, 1974.

4. J.-P. Cross-Mayrevieille, *Histoire du Comté et de la Vicomté de Carcassonne*, Paris, 1846-1896, 2 volumes. Joseph Poux, *la Cité de Carcassonne, les origines*, Toulouse, 1927. *Histoire de Carcassonne*, collective work published under the direction of Jean Guilaine and Daniel Fabre, Toulouse, 1984.

5. Yves Bruand, "Chronologie et tracé de l'enceinte 'wisigothique' de la Cité de Carcassonne", in *Mélanges archéologiques et d'histoire médiévale en l'honneur du doyen Michel de Brouärd*, Genève-Paris, Droz, 1982, pp.29-37.

6. Jean Gimpel, *la Révolution industrielle du Moyen Âge*, Paris, Le Seuil, 1975.

7. Philippe Contamine, *la Guerre au Moyen Âge*, Paris, PUF, 1986.

8. See for example, *le Dimanche de Bouvines, 27 juillet 1214*, coll. "Les 30 journées qui ont fait la France", Gallimard 1973, reedited in paperback, in the collection "Folio Histoire", 1985, and *Guillaume le Maréchal ou le meilleur chevalier du monde*, coll. "Les Inconnus de l'Histoire", Fayard, 1984.

9. R.P. Thomas Bouges, *Histoire ecclésiastique et civile de la ville et du diocèse de Carcassonne*, Paris, 1741.

10. Philippe Contamine, *op. cit.* note 7.

11. Georges Minois, "Les forteresses du pays de Galles", in *l'Histoire*, Décember 1990.

12. Pierre Héliot, "L'Âge du château comtal de Carcassonne" in *Annales du Midi*, 1966, p.7-21.

13. Yves Bruant, "Le Château comtal de Carcassonne", in *Congrès archéologique de France*, Pays d'Aude, 181st session, Paris, SFA, 1973.

14. Georges Duby, *Guillaume le Maréchal ou le meilleur chevalier du monde*, Paris, Fayard, 1986.

15. Viollet-le-Duc, *Essai sur l'architecture militaire médievale*, Paris, 1854.

16. J.-M. Carbasse, "La ville royale de la prospérité au déclin", chapter 5 of *l'Histoire de Carcassonne* under the direction of Jean Guilaine and Daniel Fabre, Privat, Toulouse, 1984.

17. Michèle Lebois, "Le complot des Carcassonnais contre l'Inquisition, 1283-1285", in *Congrès régionaux des fédérations historiques du Languedoc*, 1970.

18. Marcel Durliat, "Saint-Michel de Carcassonne", in *Congrès archéologique de France*, Pays de l'Aude, Paris, SFA, 1973.

19. Jean Rocacher, *la Basilique Saint-Nazaire et Celse de Carcassonne*, Carcassonne, 1991.

20. Marcel Durliat, "Saint-Nazaire de Carcassonne", in *Congrès archéologique de France*, Pays de l'Aude, Paris, SFA, 1973.

21. Michèle Pradalier-Schlumberger, "Le décor sculpté de la cathédrale Saint-Nazaire de Carcassonne", in *Congrès archéologique de France*, Pays de l'Aude, Paris, SFA, 1973.

22. Alan Friedlander, "Les sergents royaux du Languedoc sous Philippe le Bel", in *Annales du Midi*, t. XCVI, p.235-251, 1984.

23. In Mahul, *Cartulaire*, quoted by Pierre Héliot, "Châteaux des Pays de l'Aude", *Congrès archéologique de France*, *op. cit.*

The Narbonne Gate

This has always been the main entrance to the Cité. It faces towards the east, and the routes leading to Narbonne and the Mediterranean, and was the only gate which carts could easily approach.

1209-1240 PRINCIPAL SOURCES

Peter of Vaux-de-Cernay: *Hystoria Albigensis*

Peter of Vaux-de-Cernay was a monk from the Cistercian Abbey of Vaux-de-Cernay, situated near the Montfort estates in the Ile-de-France. Peter accompanied his uncle, the Abbott of Vaux-de-Cernay, on the fourth Crusade, which the Venetians diverted from its objective. It was during this Crusade, that he met Simon de Montfort and admired his piety and honesty. In 1212 he went with his uncle to Carcassonne, when the latter was made bishop of that town. When he returned to the Ile-de-France in 1213, he started writing his *Histoire*; at that period, this was the normal way of writing about contemporary events. He returned to the South on several occasions. His account stops shortly after the death of Simon de Montfort. It is a very subjective work; it should never be forgotten that the author's family had strong links with the Montfort family, and that Arnaud Amaury, the Abbott of Cîteaux and ''patron'' of that order, was one of the principal leaders of the 1209 expedition. Peter of Vaux-de-Cernay was convinced that the crusaders were in the right and the heretics and their allies in the wrong. However, his account is a reliable source of information, actual events are not distorted and the weaknesses and errors of the Crusaders not camouflaged. The Latin text annotated by Pascal Guebin and Edouard Lyon has been translated by Pascal Guebin and Henri de Maisonneuve (Vrin, Paris, 1951).

William of Tudèle and an anonymous author: *The Song of the Crusade*

This is a long poem consisting of 9,610 verses. The content and style indicate that there were two authors. The first third of the poem is the work of William of Tudèle. He came from Navarre and lived in the Languedoc at the time of the Crusade. William of Tudèle was a professional troubador. He may not have actually witnessed the battles himself, but he was in constant contact with the Crusaders and the local population. He probably began writing his poem in 1210 and added to it as he heard of the different events. The account suddenly stops in 1213. William of Tudèle is fair to both sides. He condemns the heretics as responsible for the outbreak of the trouble, but he also reproves the excesses of the crusaders, and takes pleasure in showing that there were courageous knights in both camps. He was well informed and careful, and can be considered as an honest historian, éven if his poetry is not of the finest.

We know very little about the person who continued the *Song*. There is undoubtedly much more life and poetry in his part of the poem. One senses that he loved recounting and took a particular pleasure in describing the exciting periods. His section, which constitutes about two thirds of the poem, was probably started in 1219 and covers the period from the middle of 1213 to the middle of 1219. Some events are ommitted, some are only rapidly sketched, others are recounted in detail. There seems little doubt that the ''anonymous'', as he is called, lived through the siege of Toulouse from 1217-1218 as one of the besieged, and it is also clear that he was a Toulouse Catholic and patriot. His sympathies lie with the people of Languedoc, but his work is an enthralling document, humane, and of real historical value, if used with discretion.

The old Provençal text of the *Song*, together with translation and notes, is published by Eugène Martin-Chabot (three volumes edited by Les Belles Lettres, Paris, 1960). Henri Gougaud has made an adaptation in modern French of the Provençal text; this version, which is not an exact translation, accurately recounts the events and beautifully renders the poetry. It is widely available in paper back (collection Lettres gothiques, Paris, 1989).

William of Puylaurens: *Chronique*

William of Puylaurens was from Toulouse and spent his life in the company of the Bishop of that town, Fulque, and of his successor, Raymond of Falga. He was born in 1200 and was still young when the Crusade began. He did not start writing his account until about 1249. He wrote well after the events, but he was well informed — he was the Bishop's confidant and often accompanied him. It is almost certain that he was with Raymond of Falga at Carcassonne during the siege of 1240.

The account covers a long period, going from the years before the Crusade up to 1273. It is not very detailed, except for certain episodes that William of Puylaurens lived throught himself or where he had solid information. He considered that it was normal to stamp out heresy, but he was not ready to condone the excesses of the Crusade, especially when it degenerated into looting and acts of petty vengeance between knights from the North and the South.

The Latin text of the *Chronique*, so called because the author had not given his text a title, has been edited, annotated and translated by Jean Duvernoy, edited by CNRS, Paris, 1976. For more information on these three original sources, the following works should be consulted:

La Croisade albigeoise, presented by Monique Zerner-Chardavoine, Gallimard/Julliard, collection "Archives", Paris, 1979.

"Paix de Dieu et guerre sainte en Languedoc", article by Yves Dossat, is particularly useful. N°4 of the *Cahiers de Fanjeaux*, Toulouse, 1969.

William of Ormes

A report sent to Blanche of Castille about the siege of Carcassonne in 1240. Practically nothing is known about William of Ormes, also known as William Dormois, except that he was Seneschal of Carcassonne. When they were annexed to the royal domain, the Trencavel lands were divided into two seneschalchies. This was more or less a reversion to the administrative organisation set up by Simon de Montfort, Beaucaire-Nîmes and Carcassonne. The seneschal was the king's representative, and as such, dispensed justice, collected taxes and maintained order. Considering the situation in Languedoc at that time, he must also have been something of a soldier as well.

William of Ormes wrote in Latin with a "French" syntax. His report is not very well structured, but there is nothing "made up" about it. Indeed, the very fact that the author was himself involved in the events and was a direct witness, lends authenticity to the account, and we can confidently rely on it. The Latin text was first published by M. Douet d'Arcq in the Bibliothèque de l'École des chartes, vol. 8, Paris, 1875 p.371-375, subsequently in the *"preuves"* of *l'Histoire générale du Languedoc* de Dom Devic et Dom Vaissette (Privat, Toulouse, 1879).

BIBLIOGRAPHY

A few essential reference works on Carcassonne

Congrès archéologique de France, 181e session, Pays de l'Aude, Paris, 1973.

Guilaine J., Rancoule G., Vaquer J., *Carsac et les origines de Carcassonne*, Carcassonne, 1989.

Guilaine J., Fabre D., (sous la direction de), *Histoire de Carcassonne*, Toulouse, 1984.

Poux J., *la Cité de Carcassonne, histoire et description*, 5 vol., Toulouse, 1927-1938.

Viollet-le-Duc E., *la Cité de Carcassonne*, Paris, 1878.

The historical context

Belperron P., *la Croisade contre les Albigeois et l'Union du Languedoc à la France (1209-1249)*, Paris, 1967.

Cahiers de Fanjeaux n°4, ''Paix de Dieu et guerre Sainte en Languedoc au XIIIᵉ siècle'', Toulouse, 1969.

Griffe E., *l'Aventure cathare en Languedoc*, 4 vol., Paris, 1969-1971-1973-1980.

La France de Philippe Auguste, le temps des mutations (report of international conference organised by CNRS, Sept./Oct. 1980), Paris, 1982.

Wolff Ph. (under the direction) *Histoire du Languedoc*, 2 vol., Toulouse, 1967-1969.

Warfare and soldiers in the Middle Ages

Contamine P., *la Guerre au Moyen Âge*, Paris, PUF, 1986.

Duby G., *le Dimanche de Bouvines*, Paris, Gallimard, 1973.

Duby G., *Guillaume le Maréchal ou le meilleur chevalier du monde*, Paris, Fayard, 1984.

Medieval military architecture

Enlard C., *Manuel d'archéologie française*, 2nd part, ''Civil and military architecture'', Paris, 1932.

Fino J.-F., *Forteresses de la France médiévale*, Paris, 1970.

Salch L., *Atlas des villes et des villages fortifiés en France du Vᵉ siècle à la fin du XVᵉ siècle*, Strasbourg, 1987.

Ritter R., *l'Architecture militaire au Moyen Âge*, Paris, 1974.

Viollet-le-Duc E., *Essai sur l'architecture militaire au Moyen Âge*, Paris, 1854.

Viollet-le-Duc's restoration work

Auzas P.-M., ''Eugène Viollet-le-Duc 1814-1879'', catalogue of exhibition of Caisse nationale des monuments historiques et des sites, Paris, 1979.

Bercé F., ''Carcassonne, la restauration de la Cité'', in catalogue of exhibition on Viollet-le-Duc, Galeries nationales du Grand Palais, Paris, 1980.

Films on the subject

The Cité was probably one of the first monuments used in films sets.

1908, Louis Feuillade filmed three short films: *le Départ pour la croisade, la Guitare enchantée, le Serment des fiançailles*.

1924, in *le Miracle des loups* by Raymond Bernard, the Cité stands for the Beauvais fortress defended by Jeanne Hachette. This film was made on a grand scale (500 actors and 1,500 soldiers lent by the army) and was a huge box-office success, both in France and abroad.

1927 in *la Merveilleuse Vie de Jeanne d'Arc* by Marc de Gastyne, the Cité represents Orléans.

Carcassonne also inspired two films:

1928 *le Tournoi dans la Cité* by Jean Renoir. This was Renoir's first long feature film. The sets which were added to the walls to complete the decor were designed by the architect Mallet-Stevens. The film was made for the two-thousandth anniversary of the Cité, and shows the Cité at its best. It is based on an historical event, the visit by Catherine de Medicis and her son Charles IX to Carcassonne in January 1565. A tournament was held in their honour. The film strays a little from what actually happened. There had been a lot of snow over the previous days and a snowball fight was held to amuse the young king.

1944 *la Fiancée des Ténèbres*, by Serge de Poligny. The monument is the centre of an intrigue, set in modern times in which the two heroes have an adventure and rediscover the ''sanctuaire des Albigeois''.

Other more recent films in which the Cité can be seen include:

le Miracle des loups, by André Hunebelle (1961),

Un Lion en hiver, by Anthony Harvey (1968),

Robin des bois, princes des voleurs, by Kevin Reynolds (1991).

GLOSSARY

Main terms for medieval military architecture:

Angle mort (blind angle): area out of the range of fire.

Appareil à bossage (stone bossing): *appareil* is the manner in which the stones are cut (size, shape) and arranged (in a disordered way, in regular layers...). *Pierres à bossage* (embossed stones) are flat on the edges but the central part comes out. To our knowledge, there is no medieval text which explains why this bossing was used. It is characteristic of late 13th and early 14th centuries military constructions in some areas of France.

Archère or meurtrière (arrow slit): slit cut into the wall for shooting. Arrow-slits seem to have been uncommon before the 12th century. They are termed *embrasées*, when the slit opens out more on the inside to provide a wider angle for shooting.

Assommoir: opening in vault or ceiling of a covered passageway, from which stones and other missiles could be thrown at the enemy, when the latter entered the passageway.

Barbacane (barbican): the purpose of this building was to reinforce the defences of the gate.

Bretèche (brattice): small construction overhanging a door or other sensitive spot; opening from which missiles could be thrown down on to the enemy.

Chemin couvert (covered way): route or way framed by two walls.

Chemise (chemise): fortified wall which surrounds the ''donjon'' or, more generally, the seigneur's residence.

Contrescarpe (counterscarp): slope of the ditch facing the enemy.

Courtine (curtain): wall or part of wall between two towers.

Créneau (crenellation): rectangular indentations in the parapet to protect the soldiers posted along the sentry-route and to facilitate shooting and surveillance.

Douve (ditch): the plural form is most often used. *Douves sèches* (dry ditches) are ditches without water.

Echauguette (watch-tower): small projecting construction on the top of the wall redan or the corners of a square tower, designed to avoid blind angles.

Escarpe (escarp): slope of the ditch on the side of the wall.

Flanquement (flanking): the towers are designed for flanking; they come out from the walls and enable the soldiers to shoot parallel to the wall onto the side of the enemy when they try to climb or mine.

Fruit : slope of the exterior side of a wall making the base of the wall thicker.

Guette : turret on the very top of a tower, for the watch.

Herse (portcullis): wooden or iron gate worked from the upper part of a door. Most of these portcullises have disappeared, but the grooves along which they ran are still often visible.

Hourd (hoarding): wooden gallery placed along the top of a wall but coming out farther than the base of the wall. Holes were pierced in the floor of the hoarding so that missiles could be dropped down on to the enemy when they were at the foot of the wall.

Lice (list): space between the two concentric city walls, or between the wall and the wooden palisade which was often put up in front of the wall. Also used in the sense of the outer wall. Plural form most common.

Mâchicoulis (machicoulis): hole through which missiles could be thrown down. Fairly wide opening positioned just in front of the portcullis, through which the enemy trying to force the portcullis could be reached. Also used to denote the projecting stone gallery which replaced the wooden hoardings along the top of walls and towers.

Merlon (merlon): filled-in part of a crenellated parapet, where soldiers could take refuge.

Ouverte à la gorge (open throated tower): tower with large opening on the side facing the town, so that an enemy who had managed to reach the tower could not take refuge there.

Palis (palisade): palisade of stakes.

Poliorcétique: the art of besieging towns, siege warfare.

Poterne (postern): small gate.

Trous de hourds, trous de boulin (hoarding put-holes): wooden beams were slotted into these holes to support scaffolding or overhanging hoardings.

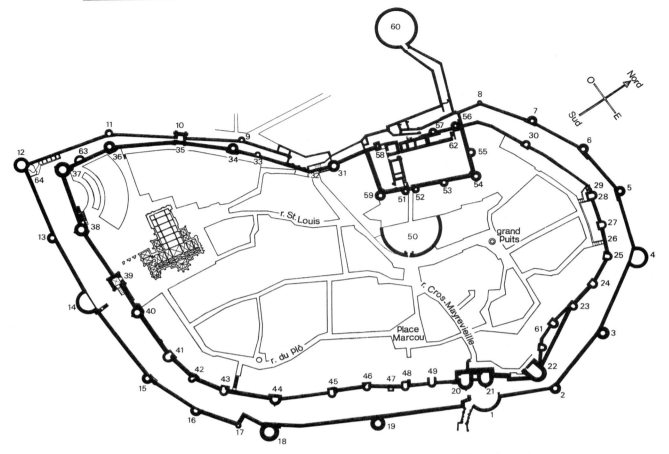

Outer Wall

1. Barbacane Saint-Louis
2. Tour de Bérard
3. Tour de Benazet
4. Barbacane Notre-Dame
5. Tour de Mourétis
6. Tour de la Glacière
7. Tour de la Porte rouge
8. Echauguette de l'ouest
9. Tour du Petit Canissou
10. Tour carrée de l'Evêque
11. Tour du Grand Canissou
12. Tour du Grand Burlas
13. Tour d'Ourliac
14. Barbacane Crémade
15. Tour Cautière
16. Tour Pouléto
17. Echauguette de l'est
18. Tour de la Vade
19. Tour de la Peyre

Inner Wall
20-21. Tours de la porte
Narbonnaise

22. Tour du Trésau
23. Tour du Moulin du
connétable
24. Tour du Vieulas
25. Tour de la Marquière
26. Porte du bourg ou
de Rodez
27. Tour de Samson
28. Tour du Moulin d'Avar
29. Poterne d'Avar
30. Tour de la Charpentière
31. Tour de la Justice
32. Porte d'Aude
33. Tour Wisigothe ou
du Four Saint-Nazaire
34. Tour de l'Inquisition
35. Tour carrée de l'Evêque
36. Tour de Cahuzac
37. Tour Mipadre
38. Tour du Moulin
du Midi
39. Tour et porte
Saint-Nazaire
40. Tour Saint-Martin

41. Tour des prisons
42. Tour de Castéra
43. Tour du Plô
44. Tour de Balthazard
45. Tour de Davejean
46. Tour Saint-Laurent
47. Trauquet
48. Tour du Trauquet
49. Tour du Sacraire
Saint-Sernin

Castle
50. Barbacane de l'est
51-52. Tours de la porte
de l'est
53. Tour des Casernes
54. Tour du Major
55. Tour du Degré
56. Tour de la Chapelle
57. Tour de la Poudre
58. Tour Pinte
59. Tour Saint-Paul
60. Barbacane
d'Aude

Excavated Remains

61. Remains of the Later Empire wall which was modified under Saint Louis, and then left behind as a result of the works carried out under Philip III.

62. Remains of a Roman house, mosaic

(probably 1st century A.C.).

63. Base of a tower.

64. Remains of a Later Empire tower which toppled over (probably during the repair work on the inner wall during the reign of Philip III).

INDEX

ILLUSTRATION CREDITS

Archives nationales : p. 59, 63.
© ARCH. PHOT. PARIS/SPADEM : p. 9, 11, 22, 24, 28, 34, 44, 65, 71, 107, 117, 118, 119.
Cartier, Patrick : 17.
© CNES/SPOT Image/1986 : p. 19.
© CNMHS/SPADEM (Lonchampt-Delehaye) : p. 85.
Mairie de Toulouse : p. 61.
Miégeville, Marius : p. 6-7, 10, 13 (coll. privée), 14 et 15 (Fonds Viollet-le-Duc, Centre de recherche des Monuments historiques), 21, 23 (bas), 31, 33, 35, 36, 37, 49, 57, 69, 73, 75 (Archives nationales), 77 (Fonds Viollet-le-Duc, Centre de recherche des Monuments historiques), 79, 83, 84, 87 (Fonds Viollet-le-Duc, Centre de recherche des Monuments historiques), 89, 91, 93, 95, 99, 101, 105, 109, 111, 112, 114, 121, 123 (Archives nationales).
Panouillé, André : p. 9 (bas), 23 (haut), 27, 53, 96.
© Photo Musée de l'Armée : p. 39, 40-41.
Roger-Viollet : p. 81, 102 (N.D.).
© Viollet (Collection) : p. 47, 66, 78.
We wish to address our special acknowledgements to the Fonds Viollet-le-Duc, for his precious collaboration.

Achevé d'imprimer
sur les presses de l'imprimerie
Istituto Grafico Bertello (Italie)

Maquette : Richard Medioni

Composition : Graphie Moderne
Photogravure couleur : Colourscan

Dépôt légal : mars 1992
N° d'édition : 63